my favorite
Cookies
from the Old Country

loved Recipes
assembled by **Olli Leeb**

Title of the German language Edition »Die feinsten Plätzchen Rezepte«
gesammelt von Olli Leeb.
ISBN 3-92179988-8 Printed in Germany
14 th Edition 1995

1998-3rd Edition   ISBN 3-921799-97-X
© Kochbuch-Verlag O. Leeb, D-80687 München
Illustrations: Kerrin v. Carnap, Icking
Photographs: Christian Teubner, Füssen
Photographs p. 10/11 Klaus Broszat München

Printed in Germany

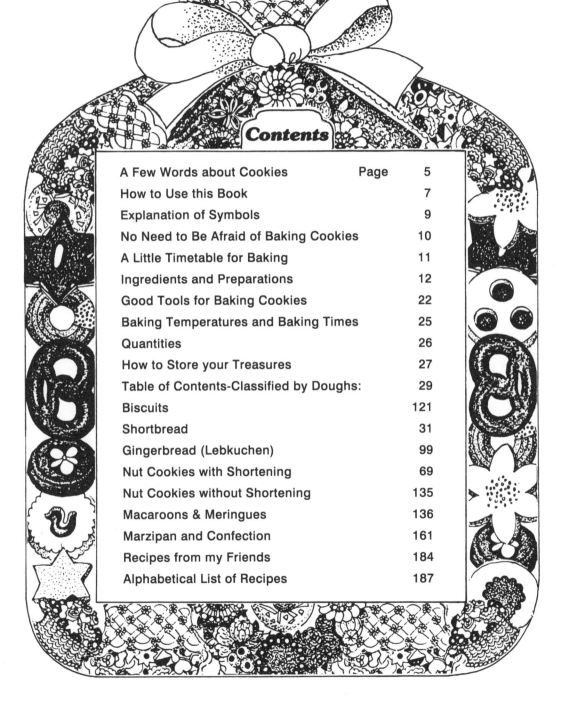

Contents

A few Words about Cookies

hat can it be that motivates people also in these days to follow the old tradition of baking cookies, Kekse, Plätzchen, Guetzli, biscuits - whatever you may call them - for festive days, especially during the Christmas season, and to make presents of them - even though it would be much easier to buy the finished products in the stores?

Is it the plesaure of shaping and decorating, the joy derived from creating your own design, which even makes you forget that baking entails some fuss and bother? Is it the longing for that unparalleled fragrance of freshly baked spice cookies which wafted through the house at Christmas time, reminding us children of the approach of merry days? Or is it the desire to make a gift of something very personal, and into which one can even bake a little bit of love?

Whatever it may be, baking cookies will never die out.
Didn't baking cookies even survive times of war, when with the most simple ingredients something special was made.

The ample supply of all ingredients enables us today to prepare all of the recipes contained in this book, being from the old days or of today, simple or very exquisite. A large part of the recipes has been collected over decades from old cookbooks handwritten by great-great-grandmothers, great-grandaunts and old friends, partly also from yellowed, grease-stained notes written in the old German script and taken out among the pages of cookbooks every year.

Originally all I wanted to do was to arrange those recipes, add the tested baking temperature and baking times, and write them down for my grown-up children ... but when everything was said and done, a book had materialized.
I hope you, too, will enjoy putting together an attractive and colorful cookie platter from these recipes- and don't forget that little bit of love!

I wish to thank Mrs. Maria Hofmann for permitting me to take three very fine recipes from her book. My thanks also go to the »Institut der Englischen Fräulein« for the permission to publish herein some of our best school recipes.

Munich, May 18, 1977

February 1978
Note on the 3rd Printing:

That baking cookies will not die out was demonstrated by the avid interest displayed by my readers, who gave me great pleasure with their friendly letters and even some of their own »sample cookies«. Some quite valuable suggestions are reflected in this edition.

October 19, 1978

Award of the * SILVER MEDAL *
of the Academy of Gastronomy of Germany

SILBER
MEDAILLE
Gastronomische
Akademie

1995 14th Printing.
1995 2nd Printing in English

According to the wishes of many friends the English Edition is now published.
After having weighed all kinds of nuts, flour, candied fruits and so on for half a year, I found out, that it is not accurate enough to provide the measures in cups.
I decided therefore to give the measures in ounces, pounds, teaspoons or tablespoons. If you want to succeed in making good cookies you have to bake by weight not by volume!
The weights within the recipes are always proportionally equalized.
I wish you lots of fun and best results!

How to use this Book

ong searches for recipes are a nuisance and will make everyone preparing to bake nervous. To make things easier, two possibilities are provided for finding quickly what your are looking for.

1. Are you looking for example, for some shortbread or nut cookies? Then open the table of contents classified by types of dough (p. 29).
2. If you know the name of the cookie you want to bake, look up the alphabetical list of contents (p. 187).

The recipes are written so that you can begin to bake right away without repeated reading. The ingredients, important for your shopping list, are indicated on the left side of the page, the preparation of the dough is described on the right side.
The * asterisk stands for ingredients which require advance preparation so that the preparation of the dough will not be interrupted e.g. that the stiff egg whites need not stand too long before »the blanched and chopped almonds« can be added. An illustration of the cookie comes with each recipe so that you will know what the finished product looks like, and enables you to recognize it in the photographs.
The recipe instructions in this book are limited to the essential direction which means that every single word is of utmost importance. If you read for instance, »the flour is sifted onto a wooden board together with the confectioners' sugar«, this has a special meaning as a flour and confectioners's sugar blend is aerated when sifted together. A wooden board also differs considerably from a plastic board when one wants to make dough with a lot of shortening. However, for other types of dough a smooth and cool working surface may be necessary.

All of the recipes are tested. Use this experience to your advantage and follow the quantities and directions for preparations closely - and the result will be cookies which you have never made before!

And now some terms which appear frequently in this book:

* **Beat in hot water**
  place mixing bowl, preferably heat-resistant, **into** a saucepan half filled with hot water. Water should not splash into bowl and should not bubble but simmer constantly.

* **Beat over - not in - hot water**
  place a mixing bowl, preferably of heat-resistant glass, on a suitable pan half filled with gently boiling water. Keep on lowest heat. Do **not** put bowl **into water**.

* **Chill**
  wrap dough in aluminum foil and chill in the refrigerator until dough hardens or is firmly chilled. (1-2 hours.)

* **Creaming**
  use softened butter and always cream butter separately first, then add one egg, some of the sugar, while constantly beating. You can cream the mixture either by hand or with an electric mixer. Watch out for the instructions when using an electric mixer!
  Important: biscuit- and meringues batter are firmer when whipped or beaten by hand. Grandma used to stir her dough 20 minutes to one hour!

* **Cutting**
  cookies are cut out with plastic or metal cookie cutters dipped before either in flour or in lukewarm water. Press the sharp edges firmly into the dough and use a rolling pin if needed. Cut the shapes close together so that there are not too many dough scraps in between. Knead the dough scraps together, wrap in foil, let rest. Important: Chill them before cutting again.

* **Greasing Cookie sheet**
  use only butter as it tastes better, even when the dough is made with margarine.

* **Egg white**
  egg white is separated from the yolk and dropped into a separate cup. Make sure that there is no trace of yolk in the egg white, otherwise it will not get stiff when you whip it. Note:
  Don't bake meringues or springerle when humidity is high, otherwise the consistency will be impaired.

* **Sifting flour**
  is important for aerating. Besides, sifting prevents lumps which form when flour gets moist.

* **Sugar draws a thread**
  boil sugar with water as directed in recipe until a thread can be drawn between two fingers.

* **Waxing cookie sheets**
  heat a clean sheet in the oven, brush on a thin layer of beeswax. Put into oven for a short time, so that the wax can spread evenly, then chill before placing cookies.

Explanation of Symbols

* asterisk before the ingredients means: prepare in advance, before preparing dough
* asterisk after the ingredients means: the recipe can be found in Ingredients and Preparations (pages 14-23)

Tbs tablespoon (level)
tsp teaspoon (level)
g gram
l liter
Ø diameter
c. cup
oz. ounces
lb pound
" = inches
conf. sugar = confectioners' sugar
= powder sugar

inch

cm

Good Tools for

large wooden

pastry board
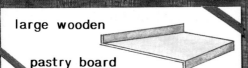

rolling pin or Pyrex rolling pin with rings for dough thickness
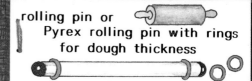

at least 2 cookie sheets

citrus-press

large drum sieve for flour

grinder for nuts and chocolate

wooden molds for marzipan & springerle
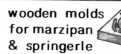

metal or plastic cookie cutters

metal shells for bear paws and...

measure table- and teespoons

syringe and icing bags

dry measure cup

pastry jagger

a set of glass mixing bowls
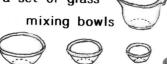

confection molds

kitchen timer
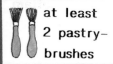

rubber spatulas

at least 2 pastry-brushes

sifter for confectioners' sugar

wooden spoons

electric mixer

kitchen scales attached to wall to keep working surface free

Baking Cookies

heat resistant glass bowls for beating in or over hot water

pastry bag with different tips for soft dough

food-mill

cookie press or attachment for grandmas meat grinder

metal spatula

platters for putting cookies on a cool place if you don't have enough cookie sheets

liquid measure jug or baby – bottle

nutmeg grinder also for lemon rind

Aluminum foil, waxed paper greaseproof paper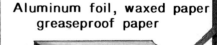

Nutcracker

small cutting board

whisk or rotarybeater

a small Pyroflam saucepan for heating icings

for storing: biscuit – tins, air-tight jars, freezing bags sealable glass screw top jars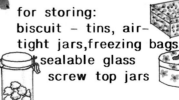

wire racks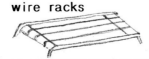

large and small knives

No Need to be Afraid of Baking Cookies

Even if you have very little time for baking, you need not forego the pleasure of baking cookies at home. If you have a deep-freezer, you are in the fortunate position of being able to bake any time you want. Besides, there are many kinds of good cookies which can be made in a very short time. When your are in a hurry do not bake cookies which need to be cut out with cookie cutters.

Instead you can:

* roll out dough, cut dough (or use jagging wheel) into stripes or rhombusses (various shortbreads).

* shape rolls or loaves from the dough, chill, slice.

* put dough through spritz-cookie-attachment of meat grinder or through a cookie press.

* drop dough onto oblaten with teespoon or pastry bag (sand cookies, macaroons, biscuits).

* make dough for shortbread, deep freeze in rolls or cut-out shapes. Bake when required, glaze or fill as directed in recipes. This way your work is divided and made easier.

The recipe part of this book includes many types of cookies, which may be shaped without much effort yet look quite different from one another so that you can arrange an attractive colorful platter. Do not make your cookies too large, for a true sign of home-baking is a delicate **small** cookie.

Use the little baking time table
on the opposite page.

12

A little Timetable for Baking

Especially for Christmas cookies, usually quite an assortment, you should have a little baking timetable. Cold and rainy November days are just right for looking up recipes, noting down ingredients, shopping, and making the advance preparations for some of your cookies.
(See p. 14)

End of November you can already bake cookies which are intended for Santa Claus and those which require storing for some time in order to become soft or to unfold their full aroma, such as Aachener Printen, Springerle, and some other varieties of gingerbread. Since shortbreads taste best when fresh, it is advisable, especially when you do your baking all by yourself, to make the dough some weeks ahead of time, wrap it in thick foil and freeze it, then shape it shortly before Christmas Day and do your baking all on one day! This will save you unnecessary stress and rush, and help you to better results. Likewise, cookies pre-cut or pre-shaped may be frozen and baked in a preheated oven without thawing. Allow a little more baking-time!

In **mid-December**, make meringues, confections, macaroons, and marzipan. Because they are so delicious when fresh, Elise's Lebkuchen, Princes Gingerbread, etc. are not due until **shortly before Christmas**.

Aside from this timetable, another timing element is important: If there is someone to share your baking with you, it will be best to have one of you prepare the dough, do the shaping and cutting, while the other takes care of the baking, spreading and filling. **Springerle, meringues and aniseed loaves** should not be baked on one and the same day, because »to dry rather than bake« may take hours when you have larger quantities. That kind of cookie is best prepared in a steam-free kitchen when the weather is dry outside, because they absorb humidity very quickly.

If you plan your timing properly
you will be able to enjoy crisp cookies and soft lebkuchen
at your leisure.

Ingredients and
Timely Preparations

Ingredients ought to be as **natural and fresh** as possible. That was probably the secret of Grandma's unparalleled success with her cakes and cookies as she never used chemicals or additives. Her spices were genuine. Butter, almonds and rum were not substituted by artificial flavoring. To make sure that your baking comes off smoothly, it is important to prepare all the nessessary ingredients properly in advance. The following list explains how to prepare them and what they are for.

* **Almonds (sweet baking almonds)**

   are used ground, chopped, shaved, slivered, unblanched or blanched, halved or whole and are available in all these forms.
   To blanch almonds: Put almonds into boiling water, let simmer 3-5 minutes. Test one almond to see if its skin can be squeezed off easily between two fingers. If so, drain, skin and spread on a cloth to dry. Dry well before storing in glass jars.
   Another method to skin almonds is:
   soak almonds in lukewarm water for 18-24 hours. Make fingertest, skin and spread them out to dry as described above. The aroma is delicious!
   Almonds can be halved more easely when they are still moist. Sprinkle the almonds with a tablespoon of sugar when you **chop** them, so that they don't jump all over the place. **To sliver**, halve almonds while moist, then cut lengthwise. If you want **to shave** almonds by hand, the best method is to cut transversely into thin slices while they are still moist. When you **grind or grate** unblanched almonds, make sure all chips of the hard shell are removed before you place them in food-processor or grinder. Dry blanched almonds well before grating or grinding, otherwise they will stick. If using a food-processor or blender take care not to overdo it. Nuts or almonds can very quickly become oily.

* **Almond oil (genuine)**
   is a neutral, fine oil; do not confuse with bitter almond essence.

* **Ammonium (ammonium bicarbonate)**
   is used as a leavening agent; rarely mentioned in modern recipes.

* **Angelica (Archangelica officinalis L.)**
  green candied leafstalks, usually cut into small diamond shapes for decorating.

* **Aniseed (seeds of Pimpinella anisum.)**
  chop finely, do not use stalks!

* **Apricot Liquor (40 % Barack Palinka) Marillengeist**
  a dry distillate from apricots.
  An Austrian and Hungarian product.

* **Apricots**
  are available dried, sulfurizied or non-sulfurized. Use top quality only.

* **Arrack**
  a spirit distilled from rice or sugarcane molasses, used for icing and as a rising agent.

* **Baking powder**
  rising agent of sodium bicarbonate and cream of tartar, mixed with cornstarch; used for simple dough. It is unnecessary when enough shortening and eggs are added. Always sift baking powder with the flour, do not mix with shortening or liquid. The dough should be baked straight away. Dough made with baking powder dries out quicker.

* **Baking soda (sodium bicarbonate) Natron**
  leaving agent for honey and molasses dough.
  Use baking soda always sifted with dry ingredients!

* **Bitter almond aroma**
  can be produced synthetically as an imitation for pure bitter almond oil.

* **Bitter almonds**
  are only used in small quantities. Keep out of the reach of children as they contain hydrocyanic acid!

* **Bitter almond oil (genuine)**
  highly concentrated, use few drops only!

* **Brown sugar**
  brown, granulated sugar mainly for lebkuchen and gingerbread dough.

* **Butter**
  always use fresh and unsalted butter. Remember to take it out of the refrigerator in time so that it is soft enough to cream. For shortbread, use cold butter, cut into small pieces. If butter is called for in recipes, do not use any other type of shortening!

* **Cardamom (Elettaria cardamomum.)**
  the ground seeds of an herb from the ginger family, typical condiment for lebkuchen.

* **Chestnuts**
  use as directed. They are sold canned or fresh.

* **Chocolate**
  for fine dough, according to recipe, grate or melt brand-name chocolate bars of different varieties over hot water.

* **Cinnamon (Cinnamomum cassia)**
  the bark of the cinnamon tree, is used ground for dough. Indispensable for cookies and cakes.

* **Clarified butter (Butterschmalz)**
  more yielding than normal butter.
  Follow instructions in the recipes carefully. Recipe to clarify butter: In small heavy saucepan melt butter over low heat. Skim off foam as it rises to surface (reserve, for example, for yeast dough). Pour clear, golden liquid into small a bowl leaving sediments in the pan. Set aside. Store in glass jar covered on a cool place.

* **Cloves**
  the dried flower bud of the clove tree is, when ground, used for lebkuchen and spice cookies. Use sparingly as it has a pungent taste.

* **Chocolate coating**
  commercial chocolate coating, sold in thick slabs, is melted over hot water without any other ingredients.

* **Cocoa**
  the best cocoa to use is the dark variety which has been barely drained of oil.

* **Confectioners' sugar (icing sugar)**
  always sift before using. Lumps caused by moisture can be dissolved in a blender or placed between sheets of foil. Crush and smooth with a rolling pin and sift.

* **Cooking chocolate**
  plain unsweetened chocolate is used finely grated or melted over hot water.

* **Coriander (Coriandrum sativum.)**
  ground, used for spice cookies.

* **Cornstarch**
  always sift before using.

* **Cream**
  use fresh sweet (heavy) or sour cream according to recipe.

* **Currants**
  very small dried blue grapes; wash in lukewarm water before using, rub dry, moisten with rum or the like. Instead of currants use seedless raisins.

* **Dates**
  prepare dates shortly before using as otherwise they lose their taste. Do not use fresh dates for baking.

* **Eggs**
  use fresh eggs only (about 2 ounces). Please weigh the eggs. If they are larger, the ratio of ingredients would not be accurate. Always have more eggs at home than you need, as eggs easely break or one can be too old. Always break open over the rim of an empty cup. Only fresh eggs separate well. Egg yolks can be stored in a cup for a few days sprinkled with some drops of water and covered with foil.

* **Egg whites**
  are best stored cool, in a grease-free jar with a screw-cap. When whipping, do not use egg whites which are too fresh. They should be stored in a cool place for at least a few days, in a screw-cap glass jar. So collect egg whites prior to baking meringues!

* **Flour**
  use all-purpose flour (wheat flour) unless otherwise indicated. Flour should be stored in a dry, airy place, and **always sifted** shortly before using.

* **Ginger (Zingiber officinale Roscoe)**
  is the rootstock of an Asiatic plant; available ground, fresh, dried or candied. Candied ginger is cut into stripes or chopped as called for in recipes.

* **Hazelnuts**
  are almost always used slightly roasted. The preferable method is to put nuts in a flat, heatproof pan, roast in oven at (325°-350°F) shake pan occasionally. Roast only until nuts begin to lose the skin. Put nuts into colander or coarsely meshed sieve. Shake so that skin comes off. This method is easier than skinning by hand. Do not roast too dark as this will leave a bitter taste. Don't grind hazelnuts in electric mixer or food-processor too long. They very quickly become oily.

* **Hip jam**
  Rose-Hip-Jam is made by mashing and stirring raw fruits or by preserving. Use as recipe calls for.

  Artificial Honey (Kunsthonig)
  use as directed in recipe. Do not use honey for a substitute unless indicated in recipe.

*   **Lemons**
    are indispensible for baking cookies. Use peel of unsprayed lemons only.

    Candied
    Lemon peel
    the candied rind of the citrus fruit is used finely chopped or cut.

    Lemon rind
    should always be unsprayed (unwaxed), suitable for consumption.
    It is used grated on sharp grater or peeled and cut in very
    fine shreds. Use potato peeler or other sharp knife to cut
    off yellow peel. Make sure that you don't cut off the white
    skin with it!

*   **Lemon sugar recipe:**
    combine ½ lb super refined sugar with the grated rind of 4-6 unsprayed lemons.

*   **Mace (Myristica fragrans)**
    ground hull of the nutmeg kernel. A very fragrant spice. Used in recipes for gingerbread and lebkuchen.

*   **Margarine**
    Do not substitute for butter or shortening. If recipe specifies margarine, use top quality only.

*   **Marzipan (almond paste)**
    available ready-packed, mix with confectioner's sugar and other ingredients as called for in recipes.

*   **Nutmeg (Myristica fragrans Houtt.)**
    the kernel of the nutmeg fruit. Use freshly grated!

* **Oblaten**
  extra thin white wafers used for macaroons, marzipan
  and gingerbread. They are either round or rectangular
  and can be bought in various sizes. Available only in delicatessens.
  When separating them use a sharp knife!

* **Obstler**
  clear liquor distilled from different fruits. (Typical Austrian product).

  Candied
* **Orange Peel**
  candied peel of the bitter orange used chopped or shredded.

* **Orange Rind**
  use the rind of unsprayed oranges only.

* **Orange spirit recipe:**
  for icing and fine doughs. Peel 4 unsprayed oranges carefully without any of the
  white inner skin adhering, place carefully into a glass jar of 1 pint 70 % proof al-
  cohol, close tightly and let stand for at least 8 days. Strain when peel has turned
  quite pale.

* **Orange sugar**
  mix ½ lb of super refined sugar with the grated peel of 4-6 unsprayed oranges.
  Store in refrigerator in screw-cap jar.

* **Pecans**
  come from the Southwest U.S.A. Are used like walnuts.

* **Pimento (Pimenta officinalis Lindl), Allspice**
  is used ground, mainly for spice cookies and lebkuchen.

* **Pineapple**
  is sold fresh, dried, canned, and candied.

*   **Pine or Indian Nuts**
    the seeds of the nut pine, use whole and fresh only.

*   **Pistachio**
    a green, small variety of almond; blanch like almonds. Protect from light or they will become pale.

*   **Poppy (seeds)**
    use ground seeds (they can be ground in food-processor). Use only fresh seeds, since they tend to grow rancid.

*   **Powdered vanilla sugar recipe:**
    Split 2 vanilla pods, scrape out the seeds, mix with 1 lb confectioners' sugar, store in tightly closed jar together with the empty pods and remove beans when they lose their flavoring power.

*   **Puff Pastry**
    available deep-frozen, thaw as directed.

*   **Raw sugar and cane sugar**
    light brown and dark, an unrefined sugar, preferable for gingerbread.

*   **Rock Candy**
    white or brown, usually used for dark spicy doughs.

*   **Rosewater**
    must not be stale. It will only unfold its fragrance when fresh. Typical fragrance of marzipan paste.

*   **Rum**
    is a distillate from sugar cane or molasses. It is used for flavoring and at the same time as a rising agent instead of baking powder.

*   **Salt**
    add just a pinch to the dough. Enhances the taste of pastry.

*   **Spices**
    never store different spices together, since they cannot hold their real magical seasoning power. For best storage, fill each spice separately into a dark, air-tight glass, away from heat and sunlight.

*   **Star aniseed (Illium verum Hook, fil)**
    fruit of an evergreen magnolia-tree, is used ground for dough.

*   **Sugar**
    use refined granulated sugar, unless different kind of sugar is prescribed.

*   **Sugar beet syrup**
    available in light and dark color. Follow directions in recipe.

*   **Sugar crystals**
    transparent, coarse-grained sugar; can be substituted with coarse sugar for making preserves.

*   **Vanilla extract recipe:**
    macerate 2-3 vanilla beans and add 1 cup of brandy, if you prefer take a liqueur. Store in glass.

*   **Vanilla bean or pod**
    available in glass tubes. The seeds can be scraped out from the vanilla bean after splitting lengthwise.

*   **Vanilla sugar**
    genuine vanilla sugar is sold in health-food stores. Can be home-made (see recipe for powdered vanilla sugar).

*   **Vanillic sugar**
    a synthetic vanilla substitute. In this book only pure vanilla sugar is used!

*   **Walnuts**
    To make shelling easier and to ensure that the kernels stay whole, soak nuts in slightly salted water for about 8 hours (overnight). If old walnuts have to be skinned, place them in lukewarm milk.
    Only fresh walnuts can be skinned easily.

*   **Yeast**
    is a biological leavening agent. Use it fresh as it perishes very easily.

Baking Temperatures

are indicated separately for each recipe. They are tested values. But since electric, gas, propane gas or convection-ovens produce different temperatures you ought to test your oven first. Bake a few test cookies made of simple dough. Compare temperatures and, if necessary, make a note of the + or – difference. This method helps you to determine the proper degrees for each recipe. If you have a gas oven, bear in mind that during peak-times, i.e. before lunchtime or in the evening, there may be fluctuations of temperatures.

The lowest level 1, in an oven operating on gas generates as much as 300°F and that is already too hot for meringues and macaroons.

Insert an ovenproof object (grater, tin or the like) between the oven and the oven door so that it remains slightly ajar. NOTE: do not use this method if you have an oven with a thermostat as it will re-heat. The safest way is to put an oven-thermometer into the oven!

Always preheat oven before baking!

Baking Times

are indicated in each recipe for the dough consistency and size of the cookies. So if you roll out the dough thinner than directed, reduce the baking time. Important: roll out or shape dough uniformly so that the cookies will brown evenly and all be done at the same time. Pretty soon you will develop the right feeling which tells you that macaroons must be soft to the touch, otherwise they will become hard. Nut- and chocolate dough should not be overbaked, otherwise it will taste dry and bitter. If the top or bottom heat in your oven is too strong, simply insert a second cookie sheet on the top or bottom shelf.

Important: Stay in your kitchen while the cookies are baking. Neither the best automatic oven nor a timer know that perhaps you rolled out some of your cookies a little thinner!

Quantities

The quantities stated in the recipes are, on the average, calculated for 1-2 cookie sheets. After long deliberation, it was decided not to indicate the number of pieces each recipe yields. For even with a precise description (in inches) considering the thickness of dough that is to be rolled out, each housewife will have enough leeway to roll out the dough a little thicker or thinner, to make the mound of a macaroon a tiny bit higher, to swirl the rings a tiny bit thicker or thinner - so any statement of quantity would not be satisfactory anyway. »So cross your heart«, who cares to count cookies when you are baking?

The situation is similar when it comes to saying how many cookie sheets you can turn out with one recipe. Different households will have cookie sheets of different sizes, some with a raised rim on three sides, some with a wider or narrower rim on all four sides! Besides, one cookie baker will place her cookies generously apart, while the other sets them very closely together. This allows for the difference of 1-2 sheets per recipe as stated above.

Note: As a rule, the cookies from the old country are small.

It's more sensible though, to add up the ingredients listed on the left side of the recipes and to allow for some weight loss with the moist ingredients. You will then arrive at the real weight of the finished product, e.g. 1 lb / ½ lb.

How to Store your Treasures

Done! Our »accomplishments«, lovingly baked, lie before us in colorful splendor, garnished with glossy icing, nuts or sugar crystals, waiting for the last act: storage. Lasting quality can be achieved only by proper storage. For that reason, please observe the specific instructions for storing given with **each** recipe.

Here are some cardinal rules:

* Allow cookies to cool completely on wire rack before storing.

* It is advisable to line tins with parchment paper or aluminum foil. Always place a sheet between two layers of iced cookies.

* Different kinds of cookies are stored separately. Delicate almond cookies, for instance, will take on the scent of other cookies. If you do not have enough separate containers, pack the individual cookies in freezing bags and store them firmly sealed in a large canister. Large jars with a lid and clasp as used for preserves come in handy, too.

* The containers should be kept in a cool and dry place.

* Some sorts of baked goods, like Aachener Printen, Honey Lebkuchen, and Pfeffernüsse, are best stored uncovered in the kitchen until soft, and later stored in closed containers. In case cookies do not become soft in time, put a split apple or a carrot into the tin, the cookies will absorb the moisture. But please check to see that the apple or carrot does not go moldy. Replace if necessary. You may also put Munich Cinnamon Stars (p. 142) into the tin of spice goods only, one day before serving, since they give off their moisture, too.

* Butter cookies **without icing** may be frozen in freezing bags or boxes while still warm. Only use the heavy bags and close tightly! Seal boxes with tape, and don't forget to label them!

Frozen cookies are thawed at room temperature and, if the recipes call for it, iced or filled. If you want your cookies extra crisp, heat them quickly in a preheated oven. Deep-frozen cookies and confection may be stored 3-4 months.

Table of Contents-Classified by Doughs:
Biscuits

Shortbread

Gingerbread (Lebkuchen)

Nut Cookies with Shortening

Almondies	72	Hazelnut Slices	96	Pecan Delights	76
Almond Rings	90	Helen's Bars	81	Spicy Stars	79
Almond Speculatius	82	Herta's Hazelnuts	81	Spritz Cookies	98
Angelica Boats	92	Ischl Cookies	95	Swabian Buns	90
Bear Paws	97	Linzer Cookies	86	Trübau Bars	70
Chocolate Bread	97	Linzer Jam Bars	75	Turkish Half-Moons	89
Coconut Blossoms	72	Millet Crispies	76	Vanilla Crescents	88
Engadine Nut Bars	85	Mock Bread and Butter	87	Vanilla Wreaths	80
Genuine Rascals	70	Mucki's Almond Slices	71	Viennese Crescents	96
Ginger Triangles	77	Nut Fingers	78	Viennese Coffee and	
Hazelnut Bars	71	Nut Stripes filled	78	Nut Buns	80
Hazelnut Buns	69	Orange & Nut Cookies	77		
Hazelnut Cookies	91	Parisian Dollars	91		

Nut Cookies without Shortening

Almond Hearts	145	Coconut Moors	138	Meringue Swirls and	
Almond Arches	145	Date Balls	146	Baskets	152
Almond Macaroons	139	Date Kisses	157	Nut Macaroons	150
Amaretti	136	Date Macaroons	151	Oat- and Nut Kisses	150
Basler Brunsli	158	Geneva Macaroons	136	Orange Macaroons	159
Belgrade Bread	151	Ginger Kisses	160	Rose Hip Meringues	157
Berlin Bread	135	Hazelnut Diamonds	147	Tuiles Noisettes	149
Chocolate Kisses	158	Hazelnut Macaroons	147	Tyrolian Leckerli	146
Chocolate Macaroons	148	Japs	137	Vanilla Chocolate	
Chocolate Rings	148	Lemon Hearts	142	Fingers	139
Chocolate Shells	140	Lemon Meringues	156	Walnut Buns	149
Choco-Walnut Squares	141	Luxemburgerli	155	Wasps' Nests	140
Cinnamon Stars Munich	142	Macaroon Bars	159	Widow's Kisses	137
Coconut Macaroons	138	Meringues	152	Zimmetsterne	141
		Meringue Eggs	156		

Marzipan and Confections

Almond Splinters	182	Hazelnut Clusters	180	Marzipan Potatoes	171
Apricot Confection	172	Heinerle	177	Mocha Truffles	183
Apricot Slices	172	Ice Confection	177	Orange Marz. Rounds	168
Bethmännchen, Frankf.	169	Ice Chocolate	177	Pinenut Crescents	168
Blackamoor Balls	179	Königsb. Marzipan	162	Pischinger Slices	178
Blackamoor Kisses	180	Macaroon Rings	169	Pischinger, Carola's	178
Carolines	181	Marzipan Buns	166	Quince Cheese	175
Chestnuts Confection	176	Marzipan Lebkuchen	166	Rum Globes	170
Chocolate Truffles	179	Marzipan Leckerle	169	Sesame Crunch	176
Dates, stuffed	168	Marzipan Mushrooms	162	Toffees	182
Florentines	183	Marzipan Paste I & II	165	Zürich Leckerli	170

Butter Roll Cookies

Shortbread

Cream in a bowl:

7 oz. softened butter (200 g)
3 ½ oz. conf. sugar (100 g)
2 Tbs egg liqueur or
2 Tbs brandy
3 Tbs heavy sour cream

add
hardboiled and mashed.
Sift onto a wooden board

*3 egg yolks

12 ½ oz. flour (350 g)

and fold in the creamy mixture, knead to a firm dough. Chill at least 1 hour. Roll out dough 1/8" thick. Cut different shapes. Place similar shapes and sizes together on cookie sheet so that they brown evenly. Rechill before baking until cookies harden. Brush over (twice) with

2 egg yolks.

Sprinkle (optional) with

sugar crystals
chopped almonds or
colored sugar
(hundreds & thousands).

Bake on greased foil until golden brown.

Bake on center rack	Temperature 375°F (190° C)	Baking time 12 min.	Store in: tin

Antler Buttons (photo p. 73)

In a small saucepan heat without browning

4 ½ oz. butter (125 g)   allow to harden in a bowl, add and stir with
4 ½ Tbs sugar (70 g)
a dash of salt
1 Tbs vanilla sugar *   until the mixture is white and foamy. Sift together
                          and beat in

5 ½ oz. flour (150 g)
2 oz. cornstarch (50 g)   knead and shape a log about 1 ½ "
                          in Ø. Chill. Brush with

1 eggwhite.   Mix:
*2 oz. almonds (50 g)   unblanched and coarsely chopped with
1 Tbs brown sugar   roll log in sugar almond mixture and pat, so it adheres.
1 Tbs sugar crystals   Wrap in foil, refrigerate until hard. Cut off slices
                          1 ¾ " thick, place slices on ungreased foil, rechill,
                          bake until light yellow.

Bake on center rack	Temperature 360°F (180°C)	Baking time 12 min.	Store in tin

Butter Flowers

Beat in a bowl until creamy:

5 oz. clarified butter
   (140 g)
5 oz. butter (140 g)
10 ½ oz. sugar (300 g)   and add while stirring
4 egg yolks
1 jigger liqueur   and the grated rind of
1 unsprayed lemon.   Sift onto a wooden board
1 lb + 2 oz flour
   (500 g)
                          fold in the sugar egg-mixture and knead. Let dough rest
                          for ½ hour in a cool place. Roll out 1/8" thick, cut
                          out flowers, place on a foil-lined cookie sheet, brush with
2 egg yolks   and sprinkle with
sugar crystals   bake until nice and golden.

Bake on center rack	Temperature 360°F (180°C)	Baking time 12 min.	Store in tin

Vanilla Moons Photo p. 93

(Vanillehörnchen, recipe from Maria Hofmann's
»Bayerisches Kochbuch« Birken Verlag München)

7 oz. flour (200 g)	Sift onto a board:
	sprinkle with
3 oz. vanilla sugar (80 g). *	
	Cut into small pieces and add
5 ½ oz. butter (150 g)	
2 egg yolks	
* 3 ½ oz. almonds (100 g)	blanched and very finely ground. Knead everything to a dough. Roll out 1/8" thick, cut out halfmoons. Chill. Let set, but not brown. Dip them carefully while still hot into
fine vanilla sugar*.	

Bake on	Temperature	Baking time	Store in
center rack	350°F (170-180°C)	15 min.	tightly closed tin

Terraces

	Loosely blend onto a board:
10 ½ oz. flour sifted (300 g)	
4 oz. sugar (120 g)	
	cut into small pieces and add
5 ½ oz. butter (150 g)	and
1 whole egg	
	knead quickly to a dough. Chill for 1 hour. Roll out 1/8", cut in scalloped rounds of 3-4 different sizes. Chill again. Bake to a light color. Use
red jelly or jam	to hold terraces together. Dust generously with
conf. sugar	and crown terraces with a dab of jelly or a
halved candied cherry.	
	Store between parchment paper.

Bake on	Temperature	Baking time	Store in
enter rack	360°F (180°C)	12 min.	tin

Orange Tongues

Cream:

5 ½ oz. + 1 Tbs butter (165 g)
5 ½ oz. + 1 Tbs conf. sugar (165 g)
2 whole eggs
1 Tbs grated orange rind
2 Tbs orange juice
1 Tbs orange spirit *
12 ½ oz. flour (350 g)

6 ½ oz. conf. sugar (180 g)
3 Tbs orange juice or
3 Tbs orange spirit

sift onto a board
blend in creamed mixture
carefully, knead to a smooth dough, chill. Roll
out dough 1/8", cut out tongues, bake until
golden. When cool, glaze with orange icing: sift
add

and stir until icing is glossy.

Bake on center rack	Temperature	Baking time	Store in
Bake on center rack	375 °F (200°C)	10-12 min.	tin

Sand Cookies

Beat in a bowl over boiling water:

8 whole eggs
9 oz. sugar (250 g)

mixture should become only lukewarm, then
beat until cold. Continue beating warming up
again and chill once more.
Melt and let cool

9 oz. butter (250 g)
12 ½ oz. flour (350 g)
4 ½ cornstarch (125 g).
3 drops of pure bitter almond
   essence or
the pulp of a halved vanilla
   bean.

sift and fold in:

Taste for seasoning with:

Press batter into small balls through a cookie-
press on a greased and floured cookie sheet.
Sprinkle with blanched, coarsely chopped
and bake until set but not brown.

*almonds

Bake on center rack	Temperature	Baking time	Store in
Bake on center rack	360°F (180°C)	10-12 min.	tin

Pistachio Tartlets

10 oz. flour (280 g)
3 ½ oz. conf. sugar (100 g)

Sift onto a board together:

5 ½ oz. butter (150 g)
3 Tbs heavy sour cream
*1 oz. pistachios
(30g)

cut into small pieces and add:

knead everything to a dough. At last add
coarsely chopped. Form a roll 1 ½" Ø, wrap in
foil and chill. Slice 1/5" thick. Bake until pale
yellow. When cool, spread one cookie with

lemon marmalade

halved pistachios.
5 ½ oz. conf. sugar (150 g)
1 tsp lemon juice
1 Tbs currant jelly.

top with another cookie. Ice and garnish with
For icing sift:
beat well with

Bake on center rack	Temperature 375°F (190°C)	Baking time 10 min.	Store in tin

Mailänderli

Cream in a bowl:

4 ½ oz. butter (125 g)
4 ½ oz. sugar (125 g)
2 whole eggs
1 grated lemon rind
*2 oz. almonds (60 g)

*ein altes Rezept
aus der Südschweiz*

add blanched and ground

9 oz. flour (250 g)
4 Tbs raisins (40 g)

2 egg yolks

sift and add:
knead lightly to a soft dough. Mix in: chopped
chill, roll out 1/6". Cut different shapes. Brush
twice with
draw lines with the prongs of a fork. Re-chill and
bake until golden.

Bake on center rack	Temperature 390°F (180-200°C)	Baking time 15 min.	Store in tin

Heath Sand

8 ½ oz. butter (240 g)
7 ½ oz. sugar (210 g)
1 Tbs milk
3 Tbs vanilla sugar *
12 oz. sifted flour (340 g)

In a small saucepan brown:
stir constantly, let cool in a mixing bowl. Add:

and beat to a white foam. Blend in:
Shape a roll of 1" in Ø in sugar crystals, wrap in wax paper, refrigerate or deep-freeze until solid. Cut off slices 1/5" thick. Bake carefully until set but not brown (except the edges). (Photo opposite page).

Bake on center rack	Temperature 350°F (180°C)	Baking time 15 min.	Store in tin

Lemon Tartlets

7 oz. flour (200 g)
3 ½ oz. conf. sugar (100 g)
5 oz. butter (150 g)

1 ½ unsprayed lemon
2 Tbs lemon juice.

redcurrant jelly

2 egg yolks
5 oz. conf. sugar (140 g)
1 Tbs lemon juice.

Sift onto a board together with
add
cut into small pieces and add the grated rind of

Rezept H. Martinetz

Knead all ingredients quickly. Shape a roll about 1 ½ " in Ø, chill (freezing compartment). Slice thinly, bake on foil. When cool, spread baked side with
and put 2 cookies at baking-side together. For icing mix and beat until quite creamy:

Store between sheets of foil.

Bake on center rack	Temperature 390°F (200°C)	Baking time 15-20 min.	Store in tin

Photo:
Heath Sand

Oatmeal Slices

	Toast lightly
9 oz. rolled oats (250 g)	in
1 Tbs butter	and
1 tsp honey.	Place onto a board.
	Cut into small pieces and add:
5 ½ oz. butter (150 g)	
5 ½ oz. sugar (150 g)	
4 ½ oz. flour (125 g)	sifted,
2 oz. hazelnuts (50 g)	ground
2 whole eggs	
¼ cup of milk	
2 Tbs vanilla sugar *	add very finely chopped
2 Tbs candied orange peel.	Knead by hand, roll dough 1/8" thick, cut into oblongs and bake until golden on a buttered cookie sheet. Spread diagonally with
chocolate coating.	Or spread dough on sheet and cut oblongs after baking.

Bake on center rack	Temperature 350°F (180°C)	Baking time 10 min.	Store in tin

Butter Bows

	Cream:
5 ½ oz. butter (150 g)	
5 ½ oz. sugar (150 g)	
1 whole egg,	
1 grated lemon rind	
1 Tbs rum	
10 oz. sifted flour (280 g).	while stirring, blend in
	Knead dough, let cool at least for 2 hours. Roll out 1/10", cut stripes ¾ x 2 ½ ", twist in the middle or pinch together. At will, brush with
egg yolk.	Chill and bake until golden.

Bake on center rack	Temperature 375°F (200°C)	Baking time 10-12 min.	Store in tin

Almond Rings

(From the »Bayerisches Kochbuch« by Maria Hofmann and H. Lydtin, Birken Verlag München)

Sift onto a board:

9 oz. flour (250 g)
3 ½ oz. sugar (100 g).   Add, in small pieces
7 oz. butter (200 g)   and
*2 raw egg yolks   and add mashed
*4 hardboiled egg yolks.

Knead ingredients quickly together. Chill dough, roll out 1/8" thick, cut out rounds and rings of equal size. Place on separate cookie sheets, because of different baking times. Chill until firm. Brush with
egg yolk
*almonds.   and sprinkle with blanched and slivered

Bake to a golden yellow. Spread bottoms of cookies with warmed
red jam.   Top with rings. (Photo p. 73)

Bake on center rack	Temperature 375°F (190°C)	Baking time 10-15 min.	Store in tin

Cinnamon Cookies

Combine and cream:

9 oz. softened butter (250 g)
4 ½ oz. sugar (125 g)
4 egg yolks   Sift and add:
1 lb + 2 oz. flour (500 g)   knead and roll out 1/8" thick, cut out as you like. Place on foil.
Chill. Brush with

egg white.

Mix and sprinkle cookies with

4 Tbs sugar crystals
1 Tbs cinnamon   and bake to a light brown color.

Rezept von Gertrude Hubert 1898

Bake on center rack	Temperature 350°F (180°C)	Baking time 10 min.	Store in tin

Mela's Butter Cookies

Sift onto a board:

1 lb + 2 oz flour (500 g).

Cut into small pieces
and add

13 oz. butter (375 g)
7 oz. sugar (190 g)
4 egg yolks
1 whole egg   knead together, chill and roll out 1/8" thick.
Cut out shapes at will. Now brush with

2 egg yolks.

Sprinkle with grated
*almonds   and bake to a golden yellow.
You can also spread the bottomside of two cookies
with
tart jam   and put them together.

Bake on center rack	Temperature	Baking time	Store in
Bake on center rack	390°F (200°C)	10-12 min.	tin

Nougat Buttons

Combine and sift onto a board:

10 oz. flour (280 g)
3 oz. conf. sugar (80 g).

Crumble with small pieces of

6 ½ oz. chilled butter (180 g)

add

2 egg yolks
1 dash of salt
1 Tbs vanilla sugar*   knead quickly to a dough. Form rolls 3/4" in Ø.
Wrap in foil and chill at least for 1 hour. Slice
thinly, bake immediately to a pale color on
aluminum foil or buttered cookie sheet.
Cool on wire rack. Melt in heat-resistent saucepan

7 oz. nougat paste (200 g).

Spread bottomside of a cookie and top it with
another cookie. Decorate with melted
chocolate coating   filled into an icing bag fitted with a small nozzle.

Bake on upper shelf	Temperature	Baking time	Store in
Bake on upper shelf	360°F (180°C)	12-15 min.	glass jars

Little Boyfriends

Sift onto a board:

8 oz. flour (220 g)

cut into very small pieces and add

4 oz. butter (110 g)   sprinkle with
2 ½ oz. sugar (60 g).   Knead to a dough with
2 egg yolks
1 tsp arrack.

Chill briefly. Roll out dough evenly to about 1/10" thick, cut out rounds about 1" Ø or form a roll, and chill. Slice 1/8" thick. Re-chill, then bake to a golden yellow. Let cool. Meanwhile quickly knead

9 oz. almond paste (250 g)
5 ½ oz. conf. sugar (150 g)   finely sifted and
some rosewater   till paste can be rolled out on conf. sugar. Cut out rounds of uniform size. Spread shortbread cookies thinly with finely strained and warmed

apricot jam.   Place a marzipan slice on top, spread with softened

chocolate coating   and garnish with
candied violet or
a small silver ball.   (Photo p. 93)

Bake shortbread cookies on center rack	Temperature 375°F (190°C)	Baking Time 10 min.	Store in glass jars

Love Letters

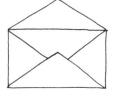

10 ½ oz. flour (300 g)
1 oz. cornstarch (25 g).

4 oz. sugar (120 g)
8 oz. butter (220 g)
2 egg yolks
1 whole egg
1 unsprayed lemon.

½ tsp redcurrant jelly.

Sift together:

Add and knead to a
smooth dough:

cut into small pieces,

and the grated rind of

Cover and chill. Roll out batches 1/8" thick.
Cut into 3" squares. In the center of each square
place,

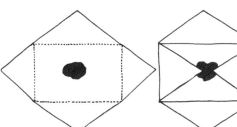

Fold squares to envelopes. Chill.
Brush with

2 egg yolks   and top each love letter with
1 halved candied cherry   for a seal. Bake to a nice golden yellow.
                               Store between parchment paper or aluminum foil.

Bake on center rack	Temperature	Baking time	Store in
Bake on center rack	380°F (200°C)	15 min.	tin

43

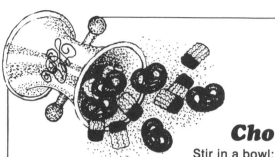

Chocolate Spritz Cookies

Stir in a bowl:

5 ½ oz. butter (150 g)
3 ½ oz. sugar (100 g)
2 Tbs vanilla sugar *
1 whole egg
1 egg yolk,

beat until creamy.

*3 oz. chocolate (85 g).

Finely grate and add

10 ½ oz. flour (300 g)

Sift and quickly blend with the creamed mixture

Chill dough. Press through meat grinder with attachment (s. p. 10) or cookie press. Squeeze out little bars, cut to the length of 2". Bake on non-stick parchment paper or foil. After cooling, dip one end into

chocolate icing (p. 114).

Let cookies dry in a warm room.

Bake on center rack	Temperature 360-380°F (180-200°C)	Baking time 10 min.	Store in tin

Chocolate Pretzels

Knead on a board to a smooth dough:

7 oz. flour (200 g)
3 ½ oz. sugar (100 g)
2 oz. butter (60 g)
2 whole eggs.

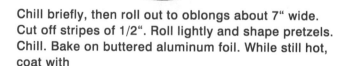

*8 oz. unsweetened chocolate (220 g.)

Grate and add:

Chill briefly, then roll out to oblongs about 7" wide. Cut off stripes of 1/2". Roll lightly and shape pretzels. Chill. Bake on buttered aluminum foil. While still hot, coat with

chocolate icing (p. 114).

Bake on center rack	Temperature 360-380°F (180-200°C)	Baking time 12 min.	Store in tin

Pig's Ears

1 pkg frozen puff pastry.

Unfreeze:

Roll out oblongs to 1/6" thickness about 3 x 6" in size. Mix in a cup

1 Tbs cinnamon
3 Tbs sugar crystals.

Sprinkle on pastry. Roll inward from both ends, not quite to the center. Cut off slices 1/3" thick. Place on cookie sheet moistened with cold water. Bake on both sides.

Bake on center rack	Temperature 480°F (250°C)	Baking time 8 min. each side	Store in tin

Streusel Bars

1 pkg frozen puff pastry
tart jam.

Unfreeze:
roll out oblongs to 1/6" thickness. Spread thinly with Cut into slices and then cover thickly with Streusel. How to make Streusel: Sift into a soup plate and mix well:

*5 ½ oz. flour (160 g)
*3 ½ oz. sugar (100 g)
½ vanilla bean.

and the pulp of

*3 ½ " oz. butter (100 g)

Melt in a small saucepan:
Cool slightly, drip into flour mixture, constantly loosening mixture with a fork. Chill briefly in refrigerator. Bake streusel bars crisp on cookie sheet moistened with cold water. Taste best when fresh.

Bake on center rack	Temperature 480°F (250°C)	Baking time 12-15 min.	Store short time only

Eder Slices

Knead lightly on a wooden board:

1 lb + 2 oz. flour (500 g)

sprinkle with

9 oz. sugar (250 g)

make a hollow into the center, add

3 whole eggs
2 small egg yolks.

On the flour ring, put small pieces of

9 oz. butter (250 g)
1 grated lemon rind
2 Tbs heavy sour cream
¼ tsp of ammonium   dissolved in
1 Tbs rum.

Knead well. Chill dough. Roll to oblongs 4 x 5" wide,
1/8" thick, place on buttered cookie sheet.

Spread with

redcurrant
jam

(which you chopped up a bit), leaving a narrow rim.
With a jagging wheel cut stripes 1" wide and place
on slabs latticelike. Pinch edges, brush with

2 egg
yolks

and bake crisp. Spread onto the visible parts with jam
the following glaze:
sift

7 oz. conf. sugar (200 g)   add
2 Tbs arrack.

Stir to a thick consistency. Cut the oblongs (while
still warm) into slices about 1" wide.

Bake on center rack	Temperature 350°F (180°C)	Baking time 15 min.	Store in tin

Aunt Fanny's Christmas Stars

Sift onto a board:

2.2 lb flour (1000 g)

make a hollow into the center, add

3 Tbs milk
4 whole eggs.

Stir in

14 oz. sugar (400 g)
7 oz. butter (200 g).

and spread over the flour ring very small pieces of
Mix, first with the knife, then by hand. Let dough
rest. Meanwhile cream well for topping:

4 small eggs
10 oz. sugar (280 g)
4 unsprayed lemons.
*10 oz. hazelnuts (280 g) or
*11 oz. walnuts (300 g)

the grated rind of
Add and fold in:

ground.
Roll out first dough 1/6" thick, cut out stars 2" Ø,
put a small ball of the nut mixture into each center,
depress with wet wooden spoon handle, fill with
Bake on greased cookie sheet until golden yellow.

firm raspberry jam.

Jam can also be filled in after baking.

Bake on center rack	Temperature 375°F (190°C)	Baking time 25-30 min.	Store in tin

Butter Loaves

Knead on a board to a smooth dough:

5 ½ oz. flour (150 g)
2 oz. sugar (50 g)
2 egg yolks
5 oz. butter (140 g)
1 lemon.

in small lumps and the grated rind of
Chill at least 1 hour and shape into small
balls. Mix:

1 egg yolk
1 Tbs sweet cream or
1 Tbs milk.
sugar crystals.

Brush balls with mixture, sprinkle with
Place on buttered sheet. Re-chill. Bake until
golden yellow.

Bake on center rack	Temperature 350°F (180°C)	Baking time 15 min.	Store in tin

Chocolate Cookies

Sift together onto
a board:

1 ¾ lb + 1 oz. flour (750 g)
4 ½ oz. cocoa (125 g)
2 tsp baking powder
13 ½ oz. sugar (375 g).   sprinkle with
13 ½ oz. butter (375 g).   Add small pieces of

Make a hollow into the center and add

3 whole eggs
3 Tbs rum
½ tsp cinnamon
1 pinch of ground cloves.   Knead together to a smooth dough. Chill briefly.
Roll 1/8" thick and cut out different shapes.
Bake on greased foil. Glaze while hot. Beat:

10 ½ oz. conf. sugar
(300 g)
2 Tbs hot water
1 tsp lemon juice
2 Tbs arrack.   Stir well until glaze is thick and glossy.

Bake on center rack	Temperature 375°F (190°C)	Baking time 10-12 min.	Store in tin

Berta Crackers

Combine and cream:

3 ½ oz. clarified butter (100 g)
9 oz. sugar (250 g)
2 whole eggs
2 Tbs vanilla sugar *
½ tsp cinnamon
¼ tsp ground cloves
1 Tbs lemon sugar *
4 Tbs milk.   Sift onto a board
1 lb + 2 oz. flour (550 g).   Knead in the creamed mixture, roll dough 1/8"
thick. Cut out crackers with a jagging wheel.
Bake until brown.

Bake on center rack	Temperature 375°F (190°C)	Baking time 10 min.	Store in tin

Falling Stars

3 ½ oz. flour (100 g)
2 oz. cornstarch (50 g)
2 small egg yolks
3 oz. sugar (80 g)
1 Tbs vanilla sugar
*2 oz. hazelnuts (50 g)
3 oz. butter (90 g)

Combine onto a board:

ground
in small pieces. Chop and blend all ingredients with a
knife, then knead quickly. Shape roll of 1 ½ " Ø, wrap
in parchment paper, chill in refrigerator. When dough
is firm, cut into 1/8" rounds, bake until light yellow on
parchment paper or foil. Let cool, then brush with

chocolate-icing p. 114

and top with marzipan star. For stars, use half of the
paste for marzipan rolls, p. 166. Roll out 1/8" thick.
Cut out stars smaller than the round cookies.

Bake on center rack	Temperature 350°F (180°C)	Baking time 10 min.	Store in tin

Parson Hats

13 ½ oz. flour (375 g).

Sift onto a board:

Add

4 ½ oz. sugar (130 g)
9 oz. butter (250 g)

in small pieces.
Make a hollow in the center and put in

4 egg yolks
2 Tbs rum

chop and mix all ingredients quickly with a knife and
knead with cool hands. Chill. Roll out dough 1/8" thick.
Cut out rounds 3" Ø. Dot center with

redcurrant jam

and pinch together in 3 places to make a three-
cornered hat. Brush twice with

2 egg yolks

and bake until golden yellow.

Bake on center rack	Temperature 375°F (190°C)	Baking time 15 min.	Store in tin

Elizabeth Sandwiches

Sift onto a board:

7 oz. flour (200 g).

Sprinkle with

5 ½ oz. sugar (150 g)   make a hollow, spread small pieces of

3 ½ oz. butter (100 g)   over rim. Put into the hollow:

1 whole egg

1 egg yolk

½ tsp cinnamon

¼ tsp ground cloves

2 Tbs rum.

Combine all ingredients to a dough. Let dough rest in a cool place for 1 hour. Roll out 1/8" thick and cut out oblongs. If you have no suitable cutter, cut out uniform oblongs with a knife. Place on sheet lined with greased aluminum foil. Brush with

1 egg white

1 hazelnut or

*1 blanched almond.   and press into every other slab

Bake slabs to a light brown, lift from foil with a long thin knife when slabs are cool. Meanwhile prepare a spreadable paste of:

3 oz. butter (80 g)

2 oz. conf. sugar (50 g)

2 oz. hazelnuts (50 g)   roasted and ground, adding to taste some

liqueur.   Spread paste onto the baked side of those slabs without nuts. Place slab with nut or almond on top. If

conf.   desired, powder lightly with some sifted

sugar.   Cookies taste best when fresh, don't store too long, since taste of filling will suffer.

Bake on center rack	Temperature 375°F (190°C)	Baking time 10 min.	Store in in glass jars

Black and White Roll

Sift together onto a board:

13 ½ oz. flour (375 g)
6 ½ oz. conf. sugar (180 g).

Add a whole cube of

9 oz. premium quality margarine
   (250g) (no butter!)

Mix and knead with ball of the thumb. Divide smooth dough into almost equal halves. Into the smaller part knead at least

3 Tbs dark cocoa
2 Tbs sugar
2 Tbs rum

Dough must be pliable and dark brown so it will contrast well with white dough. Chill both batches separately wrapped in foil.

On parchment paper roll out a long rectangular layer 1/5" thick of the white dough. On a suiting piece of cardboard dusted with flour, roll out as well, the dark dough real flat and slide onto white layer. Roll up both doughs firmly with aid of the parchment paper under the white layer. Wrap roll into parchment paper and let rest in refrigerator overnight. Then slice 1/8" thick with a sharp knife, place on cookie sheet lined with aluminum foil 3/4" apart. By all means, chill once more. Bake until set but not brown. Cookies will keep a long time but may be eaten real fresh too.

Bake on center rack	Temperature 350-375°F (180-190°C)	Baking time 12 min.	Store in tin

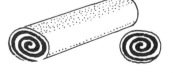

Checkerboard Cookies

Make dough as described for Black- and White-Roll, but prepare 2/3 white and 1/3 dark dough. Set 1/3 white dough aside. Cut the dark dough and the rest of the white dough into 1/3" sticks,

place on each other, alternating colors, wrap the remaining white dough around sticks to form a checkerboard. Wrap into parchment paper and chill in refrigerator overnight. Then cut off slices 1/8" thick, chill again and bake until set but not brown like the Black- and White-Roll (p. 51) (Photo p. 93)

Gay Byrdies

9 oz. flour (250 g).
1 whole egg
*2 egg yolks
4 ½ oz. sugar (125 g).
1 unsprayed lemon
4 ½ oz. butter (125 g)

egg yolk
colored sugar.

1 sugar pearl

Sift onto a board:
Make a hollow in the center and add

hardboiled and mashed. Sprinkle with
Add the juice and the finely grated rind of
and knead all ingredients to a smooth dough with
cut into small pieces. Roll out 1/8" thick, cut
out birdies, brush wings with
and sprinkle with

Into the head press
for an eye. These cookies
can be used to decorate the Christmas tree. Make
a hole into wings before baking. (Photo p. 93)

Bake on center rack	Temperature 375°F (190°C)	Baking time 15 min.	Store in tin

Christmas Trees

14 oz. butter (400 g).

7 oz. brown sugar (200 g)
3 egg yolks
3 Tbs sweet cream
1 lb + 2 ½ oz. flour (520 g)

egg white
*pistachios
colored sugar or
sugar pearls.

Stir until smooth:

Gradually add

and blend to a creamy mixture. Knead in
until you have a smooth dough. Chill. Roll out and
cut out christmas trees. Chill again briefly. Bake
to a golden yellow. While still hot, brush with
and sprinkle with
finely chopped. Decorate with

Bake on center rack	Temperature 350°F (180°C)	Baking time 10 min.	Store in tin

Filled Stars

14 oz. flour (400 g)
4 ½ oz. sugar (125 g).
2 Tbs vanilla sugar*
a pinch of mace
1 Tbs rum.
9 oz. butter
   (250 g)

redcurrant jam.

chocolate coating
1 pine nut.

Sift onto a board:
and sprinkle with
Add

Knead to a smooth dough with
cut into small pieces. Chill. Roll out 1 ½ " thick,
cut out small stars 2" Ø. Re-chill, bake to a light
brown color. Place two stars at a time together
after spreading bottoms with

Cover with
and dot each star with

Store between sheets of parchment paper
(Photo on opposite page.)

Bake on center rack	Temperature	Baking time	Store in
Bake on center rack	375°F (190°C)	12 min.	tin

Peacock Eyes

10 ½ oz. sifted flour (300 g)
5 ½ oz. sugar (150 g)
4 oz. butter (120 g)
1 whole egg
1 Tbs vanilla sugar*.

red jelly.
conf. sugar

Knead onto a board:

Chill. Roll out thinly 1/10", cut out rounds.
Make 3 small holes into half of the rounds with
your smallest cookie cutter or a vial. Bake to a
golden yellow. Let cool, then spread cookies
without holes on the baked side with warmed
Place »punched« cookies, dusted with
onto the jelly cookies. Should rest before eating.
(Photo p. 93.)

Bake on center rack	Temperature	Baking time	Store in
Bake on center rack	350°F (180°C)	10 min.	tin

Photo:
Filled Stars

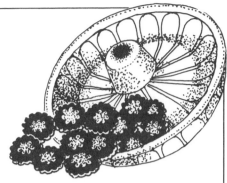

Olga Rings

(Based on a recipe from the »Bayerisches Kochbuch« by Maria Hofmann and H. Lydtin, Birken Verlag München)

	Sift onto a board:
1 lb + 2 oz. flour (500 g)	sprinkle with
9 oz. sugar (250 g)	and make a well in the center.
	Add
1 Tbs vanilla sugar * or	the grated rind of
1 unsprayed lemon.	Add
3 egg yolks	and
1 whole egg.	Cut
9 oz. butter (250 g)	into small pieces and place onto the flour and sugar. Knead everything quickly together. Roll out dough to about 1/8". Cut out round scalloped cookies and rings of equal size. Chill briefly. Bake rings and cookies on separate cookie sheets (different baking times!) to a light yellow. After cooling, spread rings with

chocolate icing.	Sprinkle with chopped
pistachios.	Spread cookies with some
red jam.	Top with iced, well-dried rings. For the icing, melt together
7 oz. unsweetened chocolate (200 g)	and
2-4 Tbs warm water.	Add
1 oz. butter (30 g)	and stir until smooth. Ice cookies at once while icing is still warm. Dry cookies in a draft-free place. Store between foil. (Photo p. 93)

Bake on center rack	Temperature 375 °F (190°C)	Baking time 10-12 min.	Store in tin

Neapolitan Tartlets

Sift onto a board:

7 oz. flour (200 g).   Add

*5 ½ oz. almonds (150 g)   blanched and finely chopped.

2 oz. sugar (50 g)

½ Tbs vanilla extract

1 Tbs lemon juice

1 egg yolk

4 ½ oz. butter (130 g)   cut into small pieces. Knead to a smooth dough. Chill. Roll out 1/8" thick, cut out rounds. Bake to a golden yellow. When cool, spread baked side with

redcurrant jam.

Place two cookies together. Cover with icing and garnish with small pieces of

*candied fruit.

For icing, stir for 10 minutes:

7 oz. conf. sugar (200 g)   with the juice of

½ lemon

2 Tbs water and

1 pinch of saffron.   Store between sheets of parchment paper.

Bake on center rack	Temperature 375°F (190°C)	Baking time 15 min.	Store in tin

Cat Paws

Cream into a bowl:

7 oz. butter (200 g).   Knead

3 oz. almond paste   with

3 oz. sugar (80 g)   and add to butter and blend well. Then quickly mix in:

9 oz. flour   otherwise dough will become crumbly. Fill mixture

(250 g)   into pastry bag and squeeze out »paws« onto a buttered cookie sheet. Chill. Bake to a light color.

Dip halfway into melted

chocolate coating   or dust Cat's Paws lightly with

conf. sugar.

Bake on center rack	Temperature 350°F (180°C)	Baking time 12 min.	Store in tin

Hawaiian Kisses

4 ½ oz. flour (130 g)	Sift onto a board:
1 oz. cornstarch (30 g).	
	Make a hollow into the
	center. Beat and put in;
2 small egg yolks	
1 pinch of salt	
1 pinch of ginger	
3 oz. sugar (80 g).	Spread small pieces of
3 oz. + 1 Tbs butter (90 g)	over the ring of flour and knead quickly
	to a dough. Form 1 ½ " roll, let rest
	for 1 hour. Slice 1/8" thick rounds
	and chill again. Now prepare the
	paste. Mix well:
4 ½ oz. almond paste (130 g)	
4 ½ oz. grated coconut (130 g)	
4 ½ oz. cand. pineapple (130 g)	chopped,
1 tsp lemon juice.	Shape into small balls and place on cookies.
	Into the center put
½ cocktail cherry	and garnish with
pistachios.	Do not overbake. Taste best when fresh.

Bake on center rack	Temperature 375°F (190°C)	Baking time 10 min.	Store in glass jars

Orange Pretzels

13 ½ oz. flour (380 g)	Sift onto a board and blend:
5 oz. conf. sugar (140 g).	Add
1 unsprayed lemon rind	finely grated. Cut into small pieces
9 oz. butter (250 g)	and blend in by chopping mixture with a knife.
	Beat and mix
2 whole eggs	with other ingredients. Chill dough. Shape like
	Arrack-Pretzels (p. 68). While still warm, coat
	with orange glaze made of sifted
10 ½ oz. conf. sugar (300 g)	stir well with
3 Tbs hot orange juice	until syrupy and glossy.

Bake on center rack	Temperature 375°F (190°C)	Baking time about 12 min.	Store in tin

Rum Tartlets

Sift and blend onto
a board:

13 ½ oz. flour (380 g)
1 tsp baking powder
6 oz. sugar (175 g)
1 dash of salt.

Cut into small
pieces and add

9 oz. butter (250 g)
2 whole eggs
1 unsprayed lemon rind

finely grated. Knead until the mixture is smooth.
Chill. Cut out rounds and rings 2" in Ø of equal size.
Chill again. Bake separately, as rings will be done
faster. Cool. Spread baked side of cookies with warm

red jam.

Place rings with dried glaze on top. Glaze for rings:
sift

4 ½ oz. conf. sugar (125 g) add
1 Tbs hot water
2 Tbs quality rum

stir for 10 min.

Bake on center rack	Temperature 370-380°F (190-200°C)	Baking time 12-15 min.	Store in tin

Bambergers

Cream:

2 oz. butter (50 g)
3 ½ oz. sugar (100 g)
½ tsp vanilla extract
3 Tbs rum
5-6 Tbs milk.

Sift together onto a board:

10 ½ oz. flour (300 g)
2 tsp baking powder.

Fold in creamed mixture. Roll out 1/8" thick and
cut out small shapes. Beat

2 egg yolks with milk

brush cookies twice. Bake to a golden yellow.

Bake on center rack	Temperature 380°F (200°C)	Baking time 7-10 min.	Store in biscuit tin

Tea Leaves

¾ pkg compact yeast (20 g)
½ cup milk.

9 oz. flour (250 g)

3 oz. softened butter (80 g)
1 dash of salt

sugar crystals

Crumble:
into

Sift into a mixing bowl:
and pour into the milk mixture.
Add:

and knead quickly to a dough. Do not allow
dought to rise. Form nut-sized balls at once and
roll out balls to thin longish leaves.
Press one side into
with a rolling pin. Place the unsugared side on a
very well buttered cookie sheet and bake until

edges are light brown. If you sugar both sides, the tea leaves tend to stick to the
cookie sheet while baking and become very sweet. Taste best when fresh.

Bake on center rack	Temperature 380°F (200°C)	Baking time 8-10 min.	Store in tin

Sugar Yeast Pretzels

9 oz. flour (250 g).
4 ½ oz. butter (125 g)

2 whole eggs
1 dash of salt.
¾ pkg compact yeast (20 g)
1 tsp milk

sugar crystals.

Sift into a mixing bowl:
Add
in small pieces.
Beat and add

Dissolve
in
and stir until smooth. Work quickly with the
other ingredients and allow to rise for only a
short time. Cut off walnut-sized pieces, roll in
Shape rectangular pretzels and bake until crisp
and light brown on a buttered cookie sheet.
Taste best when really fresh.

Bake on center rack	Temperature 350°F (180°C)	Baking time 15-20 min.	Store in tin

Stettin Cream Hearts

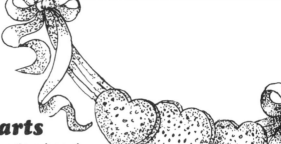

	Sift onto a board:
3 c. flour	and combine with
½ c. sugar.	Add
1 c. butter	and crumble with the flour mixture. Add
2 Tbs vanilla sugar *or	
½ Tbs vanilla extract	
½ tsp cinnamon	
a dash of salt	and
1-2 c. heavy sour cream.	Add a little more flour only if dough is sticky. Chill. Roll out about 1/8" thick. Cut out medium sized hearts, place on buttered cookie sheet. Beat
1 whole egg	with
1 Tbs heavy cream.	Brush hearts with mixture. Combine
cinnamon and sugar	and sprinkle over the hearts. Chill. Bake to a nice golden brown.

Bake on center rack	Temperature 375°F (190°C)	Baking time 10-15 min.	Store in tin

Vanilla Butter Swirls

	Sift onto a wooden board:
1 lb + 2 oz. flour (500 g)	Sprinkle with
10 ½ oz. sugar (300 g).	Add the seeds of a whole
vanilla bean	
1 whole egg	
***9 oz. almonds (250 g)**	blanched and finely ground. Knead in
¾ lb butter (330 g)	cut into small pieces. Work dough well and let it rest in a cool place. Form 2" in Ø swirls through a cookie press, chill. Bake until lightly yellow on foil or non-stick baking paper.

Bake on center rack	Temperature 380°F (200°C)	Baking time 15-17 min.	Store in tinbox

Butter Squares

Blanch and halve:

*9 oz. almonds (250 g).

Then pick out almonds of equal size and put aside. Cream:

9 oz. softened butter (250 g)
4 ½ oz. sugar (125 g)
2 Tbs vanilla sugar *
3 egg yolks.
13 ½ oz. flour
(375 g).

Sift onto a board:
Combine with creamed mixture and knead to a dough. Wrap in foil and put into the refrigerator. After about 2 hours, roll out in portions 1/8" thick and cut into 2" squares. Brush with

2 egg yolks.
almond.

In each corner place a blanched, halved
Chill. Bake until golden yellow. They are very good for desserts too. (Photo p. 73)

Bake on center rack	Temperature 380°F (200°C)	Baking time about 14 min.	Store in tin

English Crispies

Sift onto a board:
Add

1 lb + 2 oz. flour (500 g).
4 ½ oz. sugar (125 g)
3 oz. butter (80 g)
2 whole eggs.
1 tsp hartshorn salt (10 g)
½ c. sour cream

cut into small pieces. Beat and blend in
Dissolve:
in
and add to flour mixture. Knead dough well and let rest overnight between two plates. Roll out to uniform thickness, cut out shapes as desired. Press a sharp grater on cookies. Bake until crisp. No icing!!

Bake on center rack	Temperature 350°F (180°C)	Baking time 10 min.	Store in biscuit tin

Linzer Kolatschen

9 oz. flour (250 g)
3 ½ oz. sugar (100 g).
1 ½ oz. bread crumbs (40 g).
3 small egg yolks
1 tsp rum
1 unsprayed lemon.

3 ½ oz. butter (100 g)
3 ½ oz. clarified butter
   (100 g)

oblaten.

2 egg yolks
redcurrant jam or jelly.

Sift onto a wooden board:

Add:
Make a hollow into the center, put in

and the grated rind of

Cream and add:

and knead to a smooth dough together with the
other ingredients. Form a roll about 1 1/2" in Ø.
Chill. Cut off pieces to roll into balls. Place balls on
Depress the center of each ball with a floured
wooden spoon handle. Brush with
and fill with firm
Bake until golden. The cookies taste best when
fresh. (Photo p. 93).

Bake on center rack	Temperature 375°F (190°C)	Baking time 20 min.	Store in tin

Butter »S«

6 oz. flour (175 g)
3 oz. cornstarch (75 g).
3 ½ oz. sugar (100 g)
1 Tbs Vanilla sugar *.

5 oz. butter (135 g)
3 egg yolks
1 unsprayed lemon.

2 egg yolks
3 Tbs milk

Sift onto a board:

Sprinkle with

Cut into small pieces
and add

and the grated rind of
Knead quickly to a dough. Let dough rest for
1 hour in a cool place. Between your fingers roll
sticks 3" long as thick as a pencil, shape »S«, or
squeeze out dough through a cookie press. Place
on sheet lined with aluminum foil and chill. Beat

and brush »S« with mixture and bake to a golden
yellow.

Bake on center rack	Temperature 350°F (180°C)	Baking time 12 min.	Store in tin

Chocolate Kringles

Cream in a bowl:

5 ½ oz. softened butter (150 g)
9 oz. sugar (250 g)
2 Tbs vanilla sugar *
3 whole eggs
3 Tbs rum.

1 lb + 2 oz. flour (500 g)
2 ½ oz. dark cocoa (60 g)

Sift together:

and fold in creamy mixture. Let dough rest overnight, wrapped in foil. Squeeze out small wreaths
through decorating attachment of meatgrinder
or star tip of cookie press. Bake on buttered
cookie sheet. Spread ¼ of the cookie with
white icing, garnish with

colored sugar.
5 ½ oz. conf. sugar (150 g)
1 Tbs lemon juice
1 egg white.

For icing blend to a thick cream:

Bake on center rack	Temperature 350°F (180°C)	Baking time 10-15 min.	Store in tin

Hussar Balls

Cream well:

5 ½ oz. butter (150 g)
5 ½ oz. sugar (150 g)
½ Tbs vanilla extract
a dash of salt
2 whole eggs (large),
13 ½ oz. flour (375 g).

and gradually add
Knead to a pliable dough by hand, form a roll
about 2" in Ø, pinch off equal pieces and roll into
small balls. Depress in center with wet wooden
spoon handle. Brush balls with:

egg yolks.
*almonds,
red jam or jelly
cocktail cherry.

Roll immediately in blanched and chopped
fill pit with thick warmed
using pastry bag with small plain tip or fill with a
Bake on aluminum foil or ungreased cookie sheet
until nice and golden.

Bake on center rack	Temperature 375°F (190°C)	Baking time 20 min.	Store in tin

Roedl Cookies
Recipe from Mrs. Koralek, Prague

	Sift onto a wooden board, (do not use plastic surface)
2 lb + 4 oz. flour (1000 g).	Add
1 lb + 2 oz. sugar (500 g).	Make a hollow, putting in
4 raw egg yolks	
*4 hardboiled egg yolks	mashed. Cut into small pieces and spread over flour ring
1 lb + 2 oz. butter (500 g).	Add juice and rind of
1 unsprayed lemon.	Knead all ingredients quickly. Chill.

Roll out batches to 1/8" thickness. Cut out shapes. Place cutters for maximum yield, as repeated kneading spoils appearance and taste of dough. Beat

3 egg yolks, brush cookies, sprinkle right away with blanched and finely chopped

*3 ½ oz. almonds (100 g). Press in almonds lightly. Chill. Then bake to a nice golden yellow. (Photo p. 93).

Bake on center rack	Temperature 350-380°F (180-200°C)	Baking time 8-10 min.	Store in tin

Swirled Wreaths

Cream well:

5 ½ oz. butter (150 g)	
5 ½ oz. sugar (150 g)	
2 whole eggs.	Add
½ Tbs vanilla extract	and the grated rind of
1 unsprayed lemon.	Work creamy mixture into
1 lb + 2 oz. sifted flour (500 g).	Run dough through meat grinder with attachment for spritz cookies. Form sticks or rings. Place on greased cookie sheet or aluminum foil. Bake until pale golden. Dip ends into melted
chocolate coating.	Let cookies dry on a wire rack.

Rezept Hermine Antoni

Bake on center rack	Temperature 350-380°F (180-200°C)	Baking time 10 min.	Store in tin

Poppies

12 ½ oz. flour (350 g).	Sift onto a board:
3 oz. sugar (80 g).	Sprinkle with
6 ½ oz. clarified butter (180 g).	Add
1 Tbs lemon sugar *	Make a hollow. Mix:
1 Tbs cold water	
1 dash of salt	
2 whole eggs	and pour into the hollow. Work all ingredients to a dough with a knife. Knead by hand and at last add
3 Tbs poppy seeds.	Wrap in foil, chill well. Roll out 1/8" thick, cut out flowers. Re-chill on ungreased cookie sheet. Bake until slightly brown. Then glaze and sprinkle a small wreath in the center with
poppy seeds.	Top with a round slice of
pistachio.	For icing, sift
10 ½ oz. conf. sugar (300 g).	Add
2 Tbs lemon juice	
2 Tbs hot water	and tint with
red food coloring.	Stir icing until thick and glossy. The cookies taste good even without icing. You may form a roll from the dough, chill and simply cut off slices 1/8" thick, which saves a lot of time. (Photo p. 73)

Bake on center rack	Temperature 350°F (180°C)	Baking time 12-15 min.	Store in tin

Arrack Pretzels

Mix in a bowl:

5 ½ oz. butter (150 g)
3 oz. conf. sugar (80 g)
1 dash of salt
1 small egg
3 Tbs arrack.
10 oz. flour
(280 g)

Sift onto a board:
and knead quickly to a dough with the other
ingredients. Chill. Then roll out to oblongs 7"
long and 3/4" thick. Cut off little stripes about
1/5". Roll and form Pretzels. Chill. Bake until lightly
brown. While still warm brush with mashed

apricot jam.
Let dry shortly and glaze with arrack icing.
For icing, sift

7 oz. conf. sugar (200 g)   add
1 Tbs hot water
2-3 Tbs arrack.   Mix well until icing is smooth. Melt
1 Tbs coconut butter.   Beat in when cooled. Allow icing to set well.

Bake on center rack	Temperature 375 °F (190°C)	Baking time 12 min.	Store in tin between parchment paper

Albert Keks

Cream in a bowl:

9 oz. softened butter (250 g)
9 oz. sugar (250 g)
5 eggs.

Continue creaming until
mixture is light and fluffy.
Add the grated rind of
Sift onto a board:

2 unsprayed lemons.
1 lb + 2 oz. flour (500 g)
9 oz. cornstarch (250 g)
1 tsp baking powder.

Combine with creamy mixture to make a smooth
dough. Roll out 1/8" thick, cut out rounds or
even simpler, squares with a jagging wheel. Use a
grater to press in a design. Bake until light brown
on aluminum foil or greased cookie sheet.

Bake on center rack	Temperature 375°F (180-200°C)	Baking time 10-12-min.	Store in tin

Nut Cookies with Shortening

Hazelnut Buns

	Sift onto a board:
13 ½ oz. flour (375 g).	Add
9 oz. sugar (250 g)	the grated rind of
1 unsprayed lemon	
*9 oz. hazelnuts (250 g)	roasted and ground and
12 ½ oz. butter (350 g)	cut into small pieces.
	Make a hollow and put in:

1 whole egg
1 egg white
1 dash of salt.

Chop and mix dough first with a knife, then knead quickly by hand. Form a roll about 1 ¼ " in Ø, wrap in foil and chill. Slice 1/5" thick, place on aluminum foil, and re-chill. Meanwhile prepare icing with

3 egg whites (3 oz.) — whipped until they hold stiff peaks and add
7 oz. conf. sugar (200 g). — Blend until mixture is thick and creamy. Brush cookies with icing. Dot center of each cookie with

*1 halved hazelnut. — Insert an empty cookie sheet on top shelf of oven so icing won't color.

Bake on center rack	Temperature 375°F (190°C)	Baking time 10-15 min.	Store in tin

Trübau Bars

5 oz. flour (140 g)
6 oz. conf. sugar (170 g).
5 oz. butter (140 g)
*5 oz. almonds (140 g)

Sift onto a board (for 1st dough):

Add
and
blanched and ground. Crumble.
Beat

1 whole egg
1 egg white
1 Tbs water.

Mix the crumbles and knead to a smooth dough.
Chill. Prepare a meringue as follows:
whip until stiff

3 ½ oz. egg whites (90 g)
5 oz. sugar (140 g),
*5 oz. almonds

fold in
blanched and ground. Roll out 1st dough to stripes
3" wide, 1/8" thick. Spread with the meringue. Cut
into bars 3/4" wide. Place bars well apart on
ungreased cookie sheet or foil. Chill before baking.

Baked on 2 nd shelf from bottom	Temperature 375°F (190°C)	Baking time 12-15 min.	Store in tin between waxpaper

Rezept von Hilde Martinez

Genuine Rascals

1 lb flour (440 g).
13 ½ oz. butter (375 g)
8 ½ oz. sugar (240 g)
1 Tbs vanilla sugar *
*9 oz. almonds (250 g)

Sift onto a board:
Then cut into small pieces and add:

and
ground and unblanched. Knead all ingredients
quickly to a dough. Chill. Roll out about 1/8" thick.
Cut out rounds with cookie cutter 1 ¼ " in Ø and
place on cookie sheet lined with foil. Chill again
and bake after cooling, spread with warmed
and put 2 cookies together. Dip cookies in

rasperry jam
vanilla sugar *.

Bake on center rack	Temperature 375°F (190°C)	Baking time 8 min.	Store in tin

Mucki's Almond Slices

9 oz. butter (250 g)	Cream:
2 whole eggs	and
4 ½ oz. sugar (125 g).	and
½ unsprayed lemon	While stirring, add grated rind of
*4 ½ oz. almonds (125 g)	blanched and ground, and
9 oz. flour (250 g).	Knead ingredients together. Roll out dough 1/2" thick. Cut with knife or a jagging wheel little oblongs or squares. Whip until stiff
1 egg white	and coat the slices. Sprinkle with
4 ½ oz. sugar (125 g)	mixed with
*4 ½ oz. almonds (125 g),	finely ground. Bake lightly yellow.

Bake on center rack	Temperature	Baking time	Store in
center rack	350°F (180°C)	12 min.	tin

Topped Hazelnut Bars

5 oz. flour (140 g).	Sift into a mixing bowl:
5 oz. sugar (140 g)	Sprinkle with
*6 ½ oz. hazelnuts (180 g)	and
5 oz. butter (140 g)	lightly roasted and ground, add
2 small eggs.	and
	Knead quickly with dough-hooks of electric mixer or with cold hands. Fill pastry bag with the soft dough and squeeze 1" long stems onto a buttered cookie sheet. Chill. Now prepare icing: Melt in a double-boiler
7 oz. bitter chocolate (200 g).	Whip to a thick cream:
1 egg white	
4 ½ oz. conf. sugar (125 g).	Stir in chocolate. If the mixture is too firm, add a little hot water and stir until smooth. Bake stems until half done, then spread with topping and bake with reduced heat until done.

Bake 1 st shortbread on center rack with topping:	Temperature	Baking time	Store in
on center rack	350°F (180°C)	8 min.	tin
on center rack	210°F (100°C)	6 min.	

Almondies

Sift onto a board:

10 oz. flour (280 g)
3 oz. conf. sugar (80 g)
*2 oz. almonds (50 g)

and sprinkle with
blanched and very finely ground.
Combine:

6 ½ oz. butter (180 g)
3 oz. almond paste
(80 g)
1 egg white.

cut into small pieces, with

and
Knead quickly to a dough with the flour mixture.
Shape oval rolls, let them harden in refrigerator.
Slice 1/8" thick, spread with

egg yolk
*1 blanched almond
*1 halved pistachio.

and decorate each slice with
and
Re-chill, then bake until golden. (Photo opposite
page).

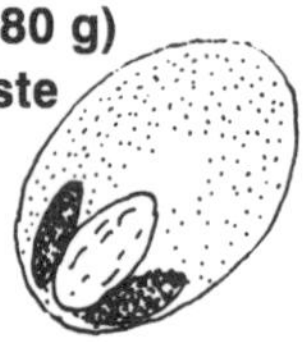

Bake on center rack	Temperature 375°F (190°C)	Baking time 14-15 min.	Store in tin

Coconut Blossoms

Sift onto a wooden board:

9 oz. flour (250 g)
5 ½ oz. conf. sugar (150 g).
a dash of salt
a dash of ginger
7 oz. shredded coconut (200 g).
1 unsprayed orange.
1 whole egg
1 egg yolk.
6 ½ oz. butter
(180 g)

Sprinkle with

Add the grated rind of
Make a hollow, put in
and
On the flour ring, spread
cut into small pieces. Work all ingredients with a
knife, knead shortly. Wrap dough in foil and chill
until it hardens. On floured board roll out dough
1/8" thick. Cut out blossoms. Chill. Bake on
cookie sheet lined with foil, until light brown.
When cool, brush only the center with

egg white
shredded coconut.
halved hazelnut.

sprinkle a small circle with
Top with a
Undecorated cookies taste also good with ice
cream or dessert. (Photo opposite page).

Bake on center rack	Temperature 375°F (190°C)	Baking time 12 min.	Store in tin

Photo:
Pekan Delights

Coconut Blossoms	Parisian Nut Dollars
Vanilla Crescents	Chocolate Carolines
Ischl Cookies	Antler Buttons
Ginger Kisses	Butter Squares

Poppies   Almond Rings

        Almondies   Colorful Spicy Stars

Linzer Jam Bars

Knead to a dough, on a board:

10 ½ oz. flour (300 g)
6 ½ oz. sugar (180 g)
*10 ½ oz. almonds (300 g) unblanched and ground,
10 ½ oz. butter (300 g) cut into small cubes,
1 egg
1 egg yolk
1 tsp cinnamon
1 pinch of cloves, juice and grated rind of
1 unsprayed lemon and
1 tsp Kirsch. Wrap into a foil and chill. Roll out half of the dough about 1/2" thick, 3" wide. Place on oblong

oblaten. Mix
about 1 lb raspberry jam (450g) with
2 Tbs lemon juice and spread dough thickly with mixture. With a jagging wheel cut off stripes 1/2" wide of the remaining dough. Place on oblongs like a lattice, brush with blended
2 egg yolks and bake slowly. Let cool. Cut into small bars.

Bake on center rack	Temperature 350°F (180°C)	Baking time 20 min.	Store in tin

75

Pecan Delights

4 ½ oz. flour (125 g) 2 Tbs soybean-meal.	Combine onto a wooden board: enriched with
	Sprinkle with
4 ½ oz. raw sugar (125 g).	Add
4 ½ oz. health-food margarine	cut into small pieces,
*4 ½ oz. pecan meat or	
*4 ½ oz. walnuts, ground	
1 Tbs pure vanilla sugar *	and
1 egg yolk.	Knead all ingredients to a dough and form an oval roll of the diameter of a pecan. Brush firmly with
egg white,	roll in crushed
linseed	and press, so linseed will adhere. Wrap in parchment paper, allow to harden in refrigerator. Slice about 1/8" thick. Brush thinly with
1 egg white,	top each slice with
1 halved pecan.	Bake to a light color.

Bake on center rack	Temperature 375°F (190°C)	Baking time 12 min.	Store in tin

Millet Crispies

	Cream in a bowl:
3 oz. health-food margarine (85 g)	
3 ½ oz. cane sugar (100 g)	
1 whole egg	
1 egg yolk	continually stirring. Add rind and juice of
1 unsprayed lemon	
*3 oz. almonds (85 g)	blanched and ground, and
3 ½ oz. seedless raisins (100g).	Mix and fold in:
½ tsp baking powder	
4 ½ oz. millet flakes (125 g).	Let dough rest for about 2 hours. Roll out 1/8" thick, cut into small oblongs and bake until crisp.

Bake on center rack	Temperature 390°F (200°C)	Baking time 8 min.	Store in tin

Orange Nut Cookies

Combine and sift together onto a board:

5 ½ oz. conf. sugar (150 g)
4 Tbs. dark cocoa
6 ½ oz. flour (180 g).   Sprinkle with
6 ½ oz. hazelnuts (180 g) lightly roasted and ground.
                           Make a hollow into center, put in

1 whole egg
1 egg yolk
2 Tbs orange liqueur.

                           Over the flour ring place
6 ½ oz. butter (180 g)   cut into small pieces and the very finely grated rind of
1 unsprayed orange.   Mix all ingredients with a long knife. Knead dough
                           quickly, form a square log of about 1 ½ x 3", wrap
       in foil and chill in refrigerator. Cut off slices 1/7"
                           thick with a sharp knife, brush with
1 egg white   and dot with a piece of
*almond.   Bake on foil or ungreased sheet.

Bake on center rack	Temperature 375°F (190°C)	Baking time 10 min.	Store in tin

Ginger Triangles »Marco Polo«

Knead onto a board to a firm dough:

5 ½ oz. flour (150 g)
*6 ½ oz. almonds (180 g)   unblanched and ground,
4 ½ oz. sugar (120 g)
1 pinch of ginger, ground
5 oz. butter (140 g)   cut into cubes. Add at last,
*1 oz. candied ginger (30 g) finely chopped.
                            Form a square log 2x2" and chill. When solid,
                            cut off 1/8" slices, halve these, brush with
1 egg white   and top each triangle with a small piece of
*candied ginger.   Chill. Bake until crisp.

Bake on center rack	Temperature 360°F (180°C)	Baking time 8 min.	Store in freezing bag

Nut Fingers

Knead quickly to a dough onto a wooden board:

10 oz. flour (280 g)
10 oz. butter (280 g)
5 oz. sugar (140 g)
*5 oz. hazelnuts (140 g)

lightly roasted and ground. Pinch off pieces and roll sticks the size of your little finger. Place on foil and bake until slightly colored. Coat while still warm with chocolate icing: Melt in a saucepan over hot water:

7 oz. semi-sweet chocolate
some hot water
2 Tbs sugar (20g)

and stir to a thick cream.

Bake on center rack	Temperature 350-375°F (180-190°C)	Baking time 20 min.	Store in tin

Filled Nut Stripes

Cream in a bowl:

3 oz. butter (80 g)
3 ½ oz. sugar (100 g)
1 whole egg.
7 oz. flour (200 g)

Sift and add
and mix well. Spread mixture about 1/8" thick on a well buttered cookie sheet, bake until lightly brown. While still hot, spread with

redcurrant jam.
6 egg whites
5 ½ oz. sugar (150 g)
5 ½ oz. walnuts (150 g)

For topping, whip in a saucepan over hot water:

until it forms stiff peaks. Blend in coarsely chopped. Stir mixture at medium heat until you can see the bottom of the saucepan. Top the jam-covered dough and bake until lightly browned. Let cool a little bit, then cut into stripes about 1 x 3".

Bake 1 st dough on center rack topped on upper	Temperature 380°F (200°C) 350°F (180°C)	Baking time 15 min. 8 min.	Store at once in tin

Colorful Spicy Stars

Blend until light and creamy:

7 oz. butter (200 g)
13 oz. sugar (370 g)
6 small eggs.
3 Tbs cinnamon
½ tsp ground cloves
1 pinch allspice
1 pinch aniseed
3 Tbs dark cocoa
1 unsprayed orange.
*8 oz. hazelnuts (225 g)
1 ½ lb sifted flour (680 g).

Spice with:

ground
and the grated rind of
Blend in:
lightly roasted and very finely ground,
Let dough rest in a cool place. Roll out dough
1/6" thick. Dip cookie cutter each time before
cutting into warm water and cut out stars 1"
in Ø. Place stars on

oblaten.

Re-chill briefly, then bake in preheated oven.
When cool, break off oblaten along the edges
and coat cookies with rose icing.

For icing, sift into a bowl:
and blend well with

12 oz. conf. sugar (340 g)
3 egg whites
1 tsp lemon juice.

Mixture should have a good coating
consistency. Tint lightly rose with some

drops of red beet juice
  (beetroots) or
red food coloring.

While icing is still moist, sprinkle stars just to
the edges with

colored sugar or
hundreds and thousands
pistachios.

mixed with finely chopped
Allow icing to dry well before storing.
(Photo p. 73). Store stars openly first, let dry
well before storing.

Bake on center rack	Temperature 375°F (190°C)	Baking time 10 min.	Store in tinbox

Viennese Coffee and Nut Buns

Mix well on a board:

10 ½ oz. sifted flour (300 g)
5 oz. sugar (140 g)
1 tsp vanilla extract.

2 egg yolks
2 Tbs milk.
7 oz. butter (200 g).

Make a hollow into the center. Put in:

Cut into small pieces and add

Form a roll 1/2" in Ø. Chill. For topping, heat in a saucepan

9 oz. walnuts (250 g)
¼ cup milk
1 tsp instant coffee
¼ cup sugar

coarsely ground or chopped, with

until paste is thick.
Slice roll of first dough 1/8" thick, spread with nut topping and bake until lightly brown. Dot each bun with a

chocolate mocha bean.

(Warm mocha beans very briefly in a pan to make them stick to the buns).

Bake on center rack	Temperature 375°F (190°C)	Baking time 12-15 min.	Store in glass jars

Vanilla Wreaths

1 ⅕ lb butter (550 g)
¾ lb sugar (320 g)
2 Tbs vanilla sugar*
1 whole egg
1 egg yolk
1 lb + 7 oz. flour (650 g)
*6 ½ oz. walnuts (180 g)

Cream well: *Rezept von Lina Kohl* 1888

Sift onto a board:
and add
very finely ground. Knead into creamed mixture until well combined. Chill. Form wreaths using a pastry bag with star shaped tip. Re-chill on foil, then bake until light yellow. While still warm, sprinkle generously with

vanilla sugar*.

Bake on center rack	Temperature 390°F (200°C)	Baking time 12-15 min.	Store in tin box

80

Aunt Herta's Hazelnuts

Cream until light and fluffy:

3 ½ oz. butter (100 g)
3 ½ oz. sugar (100 g)
2 Tbs egg liqueur
1 Tbs sour cream
2 egg yolks
*3 oz. hazelnuts (80 g)   blanched and ground.
                           Sift onto a wooden board:

7 oz. flour (200 g)   add the creamed mixture and knead well. If
                           necessary (because the egg yolks are larger),
                           add some

cornstarch.   Let dough rest in a cool place. Roll out 1/8"
                           thick, cut out with jagging wheel 1 ½ " squares.
                           Insert into center of each

1 hazelnut.   Put three hazelnut-cups together. Chill. Bake on
                           a buttered cookie sheet until golden yellow.
                           (Photo p. 93)

Bake on center rack	Temperature	Baking time	Store in
	350-375°F (180-190°C)	10 min.	tin

Helen Bars

Cream in a bowl:

4 ½ oz. softened butter (125 g)
4 ½ oz. sugar (125 g)
2 whole eggs.   Add while stirring
1 tsp cinnamon
1 tsp fine rum.

                            Blend in
4 ½ oz. sifted flour (125 g).   Spread the pliable dough on a very well buttered
                                cookie sheet and sprinkle with
*9 oz. almonds (250 g) or   blanched and shaved,
*9 oz. hazelnuts (250 g)   unroasted and shaved. Press nuts slightly down
                                with a wet wooden spoon. Bake in preheated
                                oven until light yellow. While still hot, divide into
                                bars 1 x 3". Allow to cool on wire rack.

Bake on center rack	Temperature	Baking time	Store in
	390°F (200°C)	15 min.	tin box

Almond Speculatius

	Stir until smooth:
9 oz. softened butter (250 g)	
9 oz. brown sugar (250 g).	Cream until fluffy with
2 whole eggs.	Add
*5 ½ oz. almonds (150 g)	unblanched and ground, and the following spices:

2 Tbs cinnamon, ½ tsp of each: cloves, ginger, cardamom, mace, salt. 1 Tbs cocoa and the grated rind of 1 unsprayed lemon.

	Sift and beat in one cup at a time,
1 lb + 2 oz. flour (500 g)	until well mixed. Let dough rest in a cool place at least for one hour. Roll out about 1/8" thick, dusting with some sifted
cornstarch.	Spread by rubbing slightly. Press dough into speculatius molds. Cut off excess dough directly from molds with a thin wire or a thin knife. Unmold, transfer figures on well buttered cookie sheet or non-stick baking parchment, sprinkled with thinly shaved
*almonds.	Chill briefly. Brush with
milk	and bake until quite crisp. Will stay fresh for weeks. (Photo opposite page.)

Bake on center rack	Temperature 350°C (180°C)	Baking time 10 min.	Store in tin

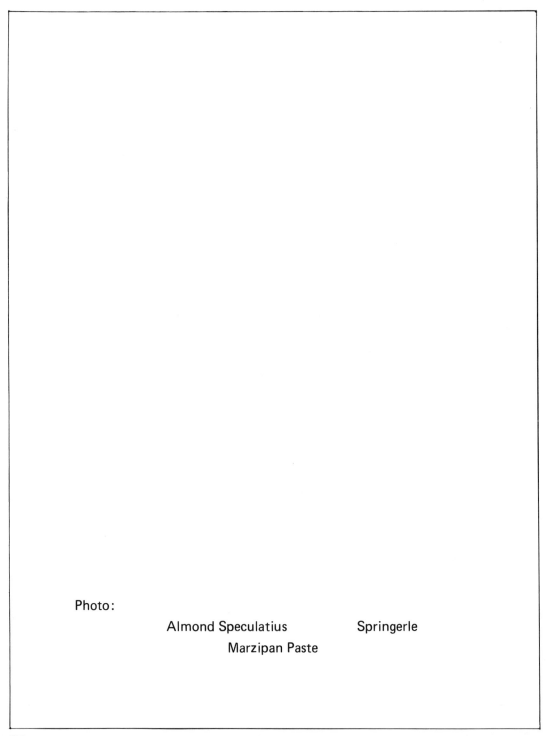

Photo:

Almond Speculatius   Springerle

Marzipan Paste

Engadine Nut Bars

Put onto a board and crumble:

1 lb + 1 oz. sifted flour (480 g)
10 oz. cold butter (280 g)   cut into small pieces,
½ tsp salt
3 oz. sugar (80 g).

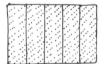

Add the grated rind of

1 unsprayed lemon
1 large egg
1 Tbs kirsch   and knead quickly. Wrap dough in foil, let rest
in a cool place.
Meanwhile prepare filling:

7 oz. sugar (200 g)
1 oz. butter (30 g)
2 Tbs honey
1 cup heavy cream.   Bring to a boil, stirring constantly, until mixture
begins to thicken. Blend in

*3 oz. almonds (80 g)   blanched and coarsely chopped,
*6 ½ oz. walnuts (180 g)   very coarsely chopped and
*3 Tbs seedless raisins   soaked in rum.
Divide dough into 4 equal pieces. Cut into slabs
of equal lengths and width, 1/8" thick. Spread
filling onto 2 slabs, leave edges free and brush with
2 egg whites.   Make a notch after every 1" (see illustr.)

Cover with remaining slabs of dough, pressing
edges firmly. Cut off stripes of 1". Brush well with
2 egg yolks   slightly beaten.
Prick with a fork. Bake until golden yellow.
Taste best when fresh.

Bake on center rack	Temperature 350 °F (180°C)	Baking time 15-20 min.	Store in freezing bags

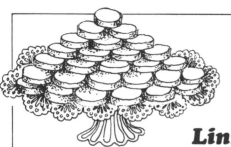

Linzer Cookies

Knead quickly onto a wooden board:

9 oz. sifted flour (250 g)
4 ½ oz. sugar (125 g)
6 ½ oz. butter (185 g)   cut into small pieces,
4 egg yolks
*3 oz. almonds (80 g)   unblanched and ground.
                                Grate and add:

1 unsprayed lemon rind
1 tsp vanilla extract
1 tsp cinnamon.

Place the dough on parchment paper, form rolls
1 ½ " in Ø, chill. Cut off slices about 1/8" thick,
place on foil, chill briefly. Bake carefully until
lightly brown. Let cool. Spread baked side of
cookies with

7 oz. blackcurrant jam (200 g)

and top with a second cookie. Ice or dust
cookies with a mixture of
conf. sugar   and
some cinnamon.

For icing sift
6 ½ oz. conf. sugar (180 g)   and
                                  add

1 Tbs lemon juice
1 Tbs redcurrant jelly
1 Tbs hot water.   Stir for 10 min.
                                 Cookies keep fresh for several weeks.

Bake on center rack	Temperature 375 °F (190°C)	Baking time 10 min.	Store in tin box

Mock Bread and Butter

2 ½ oz. butter (70 g)   Cut into small pieces:
3 ½ oz. sifted flour (100 g).   spread over
5 oz. sugar (140 g)   Add
*7 ½ oz. hazelnuts (210 g)
*3 ½ oz. chocolate (100 g)   ground,
cinnamon and cloves   finely grated,
1 egg   to taste,
1 unsprayed lemon.   and the grated rind of

*pistachios

Knead all ingredients quickly to a firm dough. Shape loaves 2-3" in Ø, wrap in parchment paper or aluminum foil. Let dough rest in refrigerator. (Dough can be prepared 1 day before baking.) Slice 1/8" thick, correct shape if necessary. Place on aluminum foil, re-chill. Bake slowly, but not too dark!! Allow to cool. Spread baked side with mock »butter«, leaving edges free. Sprinkle with chopped like »chives«. Let dry well in a warm room on wire racks.
For the »butter«, cream:

3 egg yolks
8-10 Tbs conf. sugar

(sifted) until mixture is thick and looks like creamed butter,
Bread and Butter will stay fresh for a long time. (Photo p. 113).

Bake on center rack	Temperature 350°F (180°C)	Baking time 12 min.	Store in tin between parchment paper

Vanilla Crescents

10 oz. flour (280 g)
3 oz. sugar (80 g)
*3 ½ oz. blanched almonds (100 g)

2 egg yolks.
7 oz. butter (200 g)

genuine vanilla sugar*

Sift onto a board:
and
and
not too finely ground.
Make a hollow into center, put in
Spread on the flour ring
cut into small pieces.
Form flat loaves, chill briefly.
cut off slices about 3/4" thick. With floured
hands roll slices into ropes and form
crescent shapes. Place on an aluminum
foiled cookie sheet. Re-chill and bake until
set but not brown. Dust richly with
and remove foil carefully from sheet. Lift
off when crescents are completely cool.
They taste best when fresh. Crescents can be
successfully frozen up to three months.

Bake on center rack	Temperature 345°F (175°C)	Baking time 15 min.	Store in tin

Turkish Half-Moons

	On a wooden board knead.
	quickly to a smooth dough:
13 ½ oz. sifted flour (375 g)	
9 oz. sugar (250 g)	
*9 oz. almonds (250 g)	unblanched and ground.
	Cut into small pieces
9 oz. butter (250 g)	and add
2 whole eggs.	Roll out dough 1/8" thick. Cut out half-moons with
	floured cookie cutter 2" long. Chill in refrigerator.
	Bake until just set. When cool, spread baked side
	thinly with
rose jam or	
other red jam	and place 2 moons together, cover with lemon
	icing. For the icing,
	whip until stiff:
2 egg whites	with
1 tsp lemon juice.	Sift and add
9 oz. conf. sugar (250 g)	and
2 Tbs lemon juice.	Whip until icing gets a good spreading consistency.

Bake on center rack	Temperature 375°F (190°C)	Baking time 12 min.	Store in tin between foil

Almond Rings

9 oz. sifted flour (250 g)
9 oz. butter (250 g)
1 egg yolk
¼ cup heavy sour cream.

3 egg whites
9 oz. sifted conf. sugar (250 g).
*9 oz. almonds (250 g)

Mix on a wooden board:

cut into small pieces,

Knead all ingredients quickly. Let dough rest in a cool place at least for 1 hour. Roll out 1/10" thick and cut out rings 2 ½ - 3 ½ " in Ø. Re-chill. Meanwhile whip until stiff peaks form with

Add and fold in
blanched and slivered. Spread rings with mixture and bake to a light yellow.

Bake on center rack	Temperature 350°F (180°C)	Baking time 10 min.	Store in tin closed

Swabian Buns

6 ½ oz. flour (180 g)
*6 ½ oz. almonds (180 g)
5 ½ oz. sugar (150 g)
1 tsp vanilla extract
1 pinch of salt
½ tsp cinnamon
1 unsprayed lemon.
1 Tbs kirsch
1 whole egg
1 egg yolk.

6 ½ oz. butter (180 g).

egg yolks
sugar crystals.

Sift onto a wooden board:
add
unblanched and ground,

and the grated rind of
Make a hollow into the center and put in:

Cut into small pieces and spread upon the flour ring:
Combine all ingredients with a knife, then knead quickly by hand. Chill. Roll out 1/10" thick, cut out different shapes, brush with lightly beaten and sprinkle with
Bake to a nice golden yellow.

Bake on center rack	Temperature 380°F (200°C)	Baking time 10-15 min.	Store in tin

Parisian Nut Dollars

7 oz. butter (200 g)

Brown lightly in a saucepan stirring constantly, and then put it into a bowl.

Add broken pieces of

3 oz. semisweet chocolate (80g) and mix with the butter until combined.

Blend in

3 oz. conf. sugar (80g).

Let mixture harden (preferably in refrigerator.) Then cream until smooth.

Sift and fold in 1 Tbs at a time:

7 oz. flour (200 g)
3 oz. cornstarch (80 g).

Mix in at last:

3 ½ oz. whole hazelnuts (100 g).

Chill until you can form a roll 2" in Ø in parchment paper. Re-chill. Cut off 1/5" slices with a very sharp serrated knife. Place well apart on foil, re-chill before baking, so Dollars retain their form. (Photo p. 73.)

Bake on center rack	Temperature 350°F (180°C)	Baking time 15 min.	Store in glass jar

Hazelnut Cookies

Put onto a board:

von Oma Leeb

10 ½ oz. sifted flour (300 g)
10 ½ oz. sugar (300 g)
10 ½ oz. hazelnuts (300 g)
10 ½ oz. butter (300 g)

lightly roasted and ground
cut in small pieces.

Knead all ingredients to a rich dough. Shape rolls of about 2" in Ø. Wrap in parchment paper and let harden in refrigerator. (Dough can also be prepared a few days before baking.) Then slice 1/8" thick. Bake on aluminum foil but not too dark, else they will taste bitter. Cookies are especially pretty if you brush with

egg yolk
hazelnut.

and dot each with a halved

If properly stored cookies will keep fresh a long time.

Bake on center rack	Temperature 350°F (180°C)	Baking time 10-12 min.	Store in freezing bags in tin

Angelica Boats

	Sift together onto a board:
10 oz. wheat flour (280 g)	
2 Tbs rice meal	and add
*3 ½ oz. almonds (100 g)	unblanched and ground,
5 oz. butter (140 g)	cut in small pieces,
3 oz. sugar (85 g)	
1 Tbs vanilla sugar*	
1 whole egg	and
1 Tbs apricot liqueur.	

Knead all these ingredients to a smooth dough. Wrap in foil. Chill for 2 hours in refrigerator. Roll out dough 1/8" thick, cut out little boats. Rechill.
Then bake until light yellow. Fill two boats with mashed

apricot jam and glaze with white icing.
Sprinkle sides with
*ground almonds and decorate each boat with a small piece of
*angelica cut like a diamond.
For icing sift:
10 ½ oz. conf. sugar (300 g) and add
1 egg white and
2 Tbs apricot liquor. Stir until smooth (10 min.)   (Photo p. 93)

Bake on center rack	Temperature 375°F (190°C)	Baking time 10 min.	Store in tin between foil

Photo from top left:

Hazelnut Clusters, Spitzbuebli (Peacock Eyes), Apricot slices,
Roedl Cookies, Rose Hip Meringue, Love Letter, Vanilla Crescent,
Stuffed Date, Checkerboard Cookie, Arrack Pretzel, Linzer
Kolatscherl, Quince "Cheese", Olga Ring, Walnut Bun, Little
Boyfriend, Gay Birdies, Angelica Boat, Aunt Herta's Hazelnuts,
Hazelnut Macaroon, Heinerle

Ischl Cookies

Cream in a bowl:

12 ½ oz. butter (350 g)
6 ½ oz. sugar (180 g)
*10 oz. almonds (280 g)   unblanched and ground. Add to taste
1 tsp cinnamon
1 pinch of salt   the grated rind of
1 unsprayed lemon
1 Tbs rum.

12 ½ oz. flour (350 g).

Sift and add
Knead quickly to a dough and chill.
From now on, work with only one piece of
dough at a time. Keep the rest refrigerated.
Roll out to thickness of 1/8". Cut out oval
scalopped cookies, re-chill, bake to a light
yellow. Divide the cookies into 2 parts.
Spread one part on the baking
side with the following jam mixture:
Heat in a small saucepan

2 oz. raspberry jam
1 Tbs kirsch.

Top these cookies with the bottom side of
another cookie. Coat the uppermost cookie with

chocolate icing (p. 114). or
melted chocolate coating   and sprinkle with chopped
*pistachios.   Allow to dry well before storing.

Bake on center rack	Temperature	Baking time	Store in
	350°F (180°C)	7-10 min.	tin between foil

Hazelnut Slices

Sift together onto a board:

5 ½ oz. flour (150 g)
5 oz. conf. sugar (140 g).
5 oz. butter (140 g)

Cut into small pieces and add:

*5 oz.hazelnuts (140 g)

lightly roasted, chopped or coarsely ground,

juice of ½ lemon
*1 Tbs candied lemon peel

superfinely chopped and

½ tsp cinnamon.

Knead all ingredients quickly to a dough.
Form rolls 1 ½ ", chill. Cut off slices about 1/8"
thick. Brush with lightly beaten

egg yolk.
1 hazelnut

Dot each cookie with
re-chill before baking. Do not overbake.

Bake on center rack	Temperature	Baking time	Store in
	380°F (200°C)	12-15 min.	tin

Viennese Crescents

Mix on a wooden board:

7 oz. flour (200 g)
*3 ½ oz. almonds (100 g)

blanched and ground,

3 ½ oz. sugar (100 g)
2 Tbs vanilla sugar*.
7 oz. butter (200 g).

Cut into small pieces and add
Knead quickly. Form loaves 1" high and
about 2" wide. Wrap in parchment paper and
let rest in refrigerator for 2 hours.
Cut off stripes about 1/2" from loaves, roll and
form into crescent shapes.
Bake until set (but not brown) on a cookie sheet
lined with aluminum foil. Carefully remove
foil from cookie sheet. Mix on a plate

3 Tbs vanilla sugar*
3 Tbs powdered vanilla sugar*

with
and dip warm crescents carefully into
the mixture.

Bake on center rack	Temperature	Baking time	Store in tin
	340°F (170°C)	15 min.	in freezing bag

Chocolate Bread

Cream until fluffy:

5 ½ oz. butter (150 g)
2 whole eggs
7 oz. sugar (200 g)
½ tsp vanilla extract.

Sift and beat in:

7 oz. flour (200 g)
*7 oz. nuts or almonds (200 g)   unblanched and ground,
*4 oz. fine chocolate (125 g)   grated
2 Tbs arrack.

Spread mixture evenly into well buttered 13 x 9"
baking pan. After baking, (may still be a little
soft inside) cut into 1 x 2" stripes while still
warm. When cool, coat with melted
chocolate coating.   Top each stripe with halved
*almond or hazelnut.

Bake on center rack	Temperature	Baking time	Store in
	375°F (190°C)	20 min.	freezing bag

Bear Paws

Sift onto a wooden board:
Add

13 oz. flour (360 g).
7 ½ oz. sugar (210 g)
*2 ½ oz. chocolate (60 g)   grated,
*5 ½ oz. almonds (160 g)   unblanched and ground.
                                   Cut into small pieces and add:
9 oz. butter (250 g).   Season with the rind of
½ unsprayed lemon   not too finely grated
1 tsp cinnamon
¼ tsp cloves   and the seeds of
½ vanilla bean.   Knead dough quickly. Press dough in 5 small
                                   portions into greased metal bear paws molds.
                                   Chill first, then bake in molds in preheated oven.
                                   Dust with
powdered vanilla sugar*   before serving.

Bake on center rack	Temperature	Baking time	Store in
	390°F (200°C)	15 min.	glass jar

Spritz Cookies

Cream until foamy:

10 ½ oz. butter (300 g)
9 oz. sugar (250 g)
2 egg yolks
1 whole egg
1 Tbs vanilla sugar*
a dash of salt.
*4 ½ oz. hazelnuts (125 g)

Work quickly to a pliable dough adding
sligthly roasted and finely ground.
Sift and fold in

1 lb + 2 oz. flour (500 g).

Chill. Put through meat grinder with spritzcookie
attachment. Shape into rings, »S« or small
sticks. Re-chill (very important) on buttered
cookie sheet or foil. Bake until lightly brown.
After baking, dip ends into melted

chocolate coating.

Let dry in a warm room.

Bake on center rack	Temperature 375°F (190°C)	Baking time 10-15 min.	Store in tin

Gingerbread (Lebkuchen)

Brownies

Heat slightly in a large saucepan:

3 Tbs honey
1 lb + 3 Tbs brown sugar (480 g). Add
4 whole eggs and cream mixture very well.
Stir in:

*6 Tbs candied lemon peel (60 g)
*6 Tbs candied orange peel (60 g) very finely chopped,
*3 oz. walnuts (80 g) chopped
*2 ½ oz. almonds (60 g) ground. Season
mixture with:

1 Tbs cinnamon
½ tsp cloves
½ tsp mace. Sift together and fold into the creamy
mixture:

1 lb + 2 oz. flour (500 g)
1 tsp baking soda. Let dough rest until small balls of 1" in Ø can
be formed with moist hands. If dough seems
to be too soft, let it rest (covered) for some
more hours at room temperature.
Then place balls well apart on a cookie sheet
lined with foil. Mix
2 Tbs honey with
1 Tbs hot water and brush cookies with mixture. Return briefly
into oven. Before storing, keep them un-
covered in the kitchen for some days.

Bake on center rack	Temperature 350°-360°F (170-180°C)		Baking time 15 min.	Store in tin

Gingerbread

6 ½ oz. sugar (180 g)
1 lb + 2 oz. honey (500 g).

5 ½ oz. butter (155 g)
2 Tbs lard
1 whole egg
1 egg yolk
1 Tbs cinnamon
1 tsp cardamom
1 tsp cloves
½ tsp allspice
1 Tbs cocoa.
1 Tbs potash
1 jigger kirsch

1 lb + 2 oz. rye flour (500 g)
1 lb + 2 oz. wheat flour (500 g).

Dissolve over
low heat:
in
Cool only slightly and
stir in:

For piping:
9 oz. conf. sugar (250 g)
1 egg white
1 Tbs lemon juice
cream until stiff
add food coloring.

Dissolve
in
and combine with batter.
Sift onto a board:

almonds or hazelnuts.

Add creamed mixture and knead until dough is
quite smooth. Let rest in a bowl, covered with a
cloth, in a warm room for about ten days.
(Or even longer). Re-knead dough. Roll out
one piece at a time 1/2" thick. Cut out figures
and bake on buttered cookie sheet. When
cooled, decorate attractively with white
icing using piping bag. Dough may
also be cut into oblongs decorated with
Let stand uncovered before storing.

Bake on center rack	Temperature 345°F (175°C)	Baking time 20 min.	Store in tin in freezing bags

Lebkuchen Hearts

Heat slowly in a large saucepan:

12 ½ oz. artificial honey (350 g)
9 oz. sugar (250 g).

Let cool until lukewarm and add:

3 whole eggs
3 oz. cocoa (80 g)
*7 oz. hazelnuts (200 g)

lightly roasted and ground. Beat well.
Season with:

2 Tbs vanilla sugar*
1 Tbs cinnamon
1 tsp cloves
1 pinch of mace
1 pinch of cardamom.   Add
1 tsp hartshorn salt   dissolved in
2 Tbs water.   Onto a board sift:
1 ½ lb + 2 oz. flour (750 g).   Make a hollow into the center, put in creamed
mixture and knead well. Roll out dough about
1/5" thick, cut out hearts about 5". Place on well buttered cookie sheet or
aluminum foil, dusted with flour. Let dry overnight. Bake. Let cool and coat with
chocolate icing p. 114. Decorate with white or pink piping.

For piping whip:
1 small egg white   until very stiff. Sift and add
½ tsp Lemonjuice
5 ½ oz. conf. sugar (155 g)   and stir until very thick (add more
conf. sugar if necessary).
The icing may be colored with red food coloring, the juice of a red beet or some
saffron for yellow color. Make your own decorating bag from parchment paper.
Fill in icing, cut off tip, press and draw designs. (Photo p. 103)

Bake on center rack	Temperature	Baking time	Store in
Bake on center rack	350°F (180°C)	15-20 min.	card board box

Honey Lebkuchen

Heat slowly in a saucepan:

9 oz. honey (250 g) or
9 oz artificial honey (250 g).   Allow to cool until lukewarm.
Meanwhile cream well in a bowl:

5 whole eggs
1 lb + 2 oz. sugar (500 g)
3 Tbs cinnamon
1 tsp cloves
1 tsp mace
1 tsp cardamom   the grated rind of
2 unsprayed lemons   and of
1 unsprayed orange
1 tsp potash   dissolved in
1 Tbs rosewater.   Add the honey mixture and beat until well
combined. Sift onto a board
1 ½ lb + 6 oz. flour (850 g)   mix and knead with batter until dough is
smooth. Cut out different shapes the size of
playing cards and decorate with
almonds.   Place on
oblaten.   Cover lightly with a cloth and bake the next day.
While still warm, glaze lebkuchen or decorate
with white or colored icing.
For glaze, boil:

7 oz. sugar (200 g)
½ cup water   until sugar draws a thread between two fingers.
Icing for piping: whip until stiff

1 egg white
1 Tbs lemon juice.   Add
7 oz. conf. sugar (200 g)   and beat until mixture is thick and of a white
foamy consistency. (10-15 min.) If desired, tint
with
food coloring.   (Photo opposite page).

Bake on center rack	Temperature	Baking time	Store in
Bake on center rack	Temperature 390°F (200 °C)	Baking time 20 min.	Store in card board box

Photo:

Honey Lebkuchen   Cobblestones   Aachener Printen

Lebkuchen Hearts

Augsburg Christmas Cookies

Cream in a large bowl until foamy:

9 oz. sugar (250 g)
2 whole eggs
2 Tbs honey
*3 Tbs candied lemon peel   and
*3 Tbs candied orange peel   very finely chopped.
                               Season with

2 Tbs cinnamon
1 tsp cloves.   Blend in
*4 ½ oz. almonds (125 g)   blanched and chopped. Sift and fold in
10 ½ oz. flour (300 g).   Dissolve
1 tsp hartshorn salt   in
1 Tbs water   and knead into the dough. Let dough rest over-
                               night. Then roll out on buttered cookie sheet.
                               Bake. Cut while still warm, 3 x 1" stripes and
                               glaze. You can also cut out different shapes
                               before baking. For icing, sift

4 ½ oz. conf. sugar (125 g)   whip with
1 tsp lemon juice   and
1 egg white.   Coat cookies. Let dry in lukewarm oven.

Bake on center rack	Temperature 350°F (180°C)	Baking time 12 min.	Store in tin in freezing bag

Hazelnut Lebkuchen

Beat over - not in - hot water until foamy:

3 whole eggs
7 oz. sugar (200 g)
2 Tbs vanilla sugar*
2 Tbs rum
1 tsp cinnamon
a dash of cloves
a dash of ground aniseed.   Add and combine
*8 Tbs candied lemon peel (80 g)
*10 ½ oz. hazelnuts (300 g)   ground.
                               If dough seems too soft, let rest for some hours.
                               Spread mixture 1/2" thick on rectangular
oblaten 2 x 3".   Flatten edges and garnish each piece with
1 whole hazelnut   and little stripes of
candied lemon peel.   Bake slowly. If you bake in gas oven, leave door ajar.

Bake on center rack	Temperature 320°F (160°C)	Baking time 20 min.	Store in tin in freezing bag

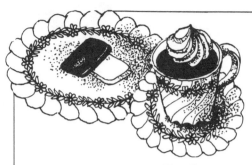

Princes Gingerbread

5 ½ oz. butter (150 g).	Melt in a heat resistant bowl When lukewarm, cream with
10 ½ oz. sugar (300 g)	
3 large eggs	
3 Tbs cocoa	
1 Tbs cinnamon	and
a pinch of clove	until mixture is very foamy. Add and fold in:
*3 ½ oz. candied lemon peel (100 g)	very finely chopped
*3 ½ oz. candied orange peel (100 g)	very finely chopped
*7 oz. hazelnuts (200 g)	lightly roasted and ground,
*3 ½ oz. currants (100 g) or 3 ½ oz. seedless raisins (100 g)	washed and drained, and
1 cup milk.	
	Sift together and beat in until well combined:
1 lb + 2 oz. flour (500 g)	
1 ½ Tbs baking powder.	Spread about 1/3" thick on rectangular
oblaten.	Cut lengthwise in 1 ¼ x 4" stripes. After baking, allow the first part of the bars to cool. Later coat with melted
7 oz. semisweet chocolate.	
	Glaze the other part while still hot. For glaze, blend
8 oz. sugar (225 g)	and
½ cup water.	Heat slowly and boil until sugar draws a thread between two fingers.

Bake on center rack	Temperature 350°F (180°C)	Baking time 15-20 min.	Store in tin

Cobblestones

	Melt over low heat,
9 oz. honey (250 g).	Add and beat in:
3 oz. sugar (80 g)	
½ Tbs vanilla extract	
a dash of salt	and
3 oz. lard (80 g).	Spice with
2 Tbs cinnamon	
½ tsp allspice	and the grated rind of
2 unsprayed lemons.	
	Add
1 egg	and stir in until well mixed:
*4 ½ oz. hazelnuts (125 g)	ground and
*6 Tbs candied orange peel	finely chopped.
(60 g)	Sift together onto a board:
1 lb + 2 oz. flour (500 g)	
1 tsp baking soda.	Knead to a dough with honey mixture. Shape

Knead to a dough with honey mixture. Shape rolls the size of your small finger, cut off pieces and shape hazelnut sized balls. Place closely together in tin rings or aluminum molds about 3" in Ø. Bake. Coat with white icing while still hot. For icing: whip until stiff

2 egg whites
1 Tbs lemon juice.   Add and beat in gradually until glossy:
1 Tbs rum
7 oz. conf. sugar (200 g)   If necessary, add some drops of water.
                            Icing should be transparent enough to let
                            cobblestones shine through. Let dry uncovered
                            before storing.

Bake on center rack	Temperature 350°F (180°C)	Baking time 15-20 min.	Store in tin

Nuremberg Spice Cookies

Beat until very foamy:

3 whole eggs (6 ½ oz.)
14 oz. dark brown sugar (400 g) and
4 ½ oz. honey (125 g)

for about 15 min. (longer by hand).
Add:

*8 Tbs. candied lemon peel finely chopped
*8 Tbs. candied orange peel finely chopped
*3 oz. hazelnuts (80 g) coarsely chopped
2 Tbs cinnamon
1 tsp cardamom and
1 tsp cloves.

Dissolve and add
1 Tbs hartshorn salt in
2 Tbs water.

Sift and beat in, until well mixed,
1 lb + 3 oz. flour (530 g). Leave covered overnight or longer. Place
cherry-sized balls well apart on buttered and
flour - dusted cookie sheet. Bake not too dry.
After baking, heat

3 Tbs honey with
2 Tbs hot water. Glaze cookies with mixture, return to oven
briefly. Store, first uncovered in kitchen, before
storing in tin. (Photo p. 113).

Bake on center rack	Temperature 340°F (170°C)	Baking time 10-15 min.	Store in tin in freezing bag

Chocolate Gingerbread

Melt and combine over low heat:

7 oz. honey (200 g)
6 oz. sugar (160 g)
4 oz. chocolate (120 g)

broken into pieces.
Add and fold in:

*5 Tbs candied orange peel (50 g)
*3 ½ oz. hazelnuts (100 g)
*3 ½ oz. hazelnuts (100 g)
1 Tbs cinnamon
½ tsp ginger
½ tsp cloves
1 tsp cardamom
2 whole eggs
2 Tbs rum.
12 ½ oz. flour (350 g)
1 Tbs baking soda.
rectangular oblaten.

finely chopped
lightly roasted and ground
lightly roasted and halved

and
Sift together and fold in:

Spread dough 1/2" thick on
Cut into 4 oblongs and bake right away.
While still warm, cover with melted

chocolate coating or
chocolate icing p. 114.

Bake on center rack	Temperature	Baking time	Store in
	350°F(180°C)	30-40 min.	tin

Quick Printen

Melt over low heat and let cool

1 lb + 2 oz. artificial honey
    (500 g).

Combine and sift onto a board:

1 lb + 2 oz. flour (500 g)
1 Tbs baking powder.

Make a hollow into center placing in

2 whole eggs
4 ½ oz. butter (125 g)

cut into small pieces, sprinkle
with
Add the artificial honey, the grated rind of

7 oz. sugar (200 g).
1 unsprayed lemon
*3 Tbs candied orange peel
*2 oz. walnuts (50 g)
2 Tbs rum.
1 Tbs cinnamon
½ tsp cloves
a pinch of cardamom
a pinch of mace.

finely chopped
ground and
Season with:

and
Knead well to a firm dough, roll out 1/8" thick
and cut out 3 x 1" bars with jagging wheel.
Bake on well buttered cookie sheet. After
baking, glaze with arrack icing.
For arrack icing, sift:

7 oz. conf. sugar (200 g)
1 Tbs hot water
½ tsp vinegar
about 2 Tbs arrack.

and add

Beat very well.

Bake on center rack	Temperature	Baking time	Store in
Bake on center rack	360-375°F (180-190°C)	10-15 min.	tin

Pfeffernüsse

	Cream until foamy:
6 egg yolks	
1 ¼ lb sugar (580 g).	Mixture must be light and fluffy.
	Whip until very stiff,
5 egg whites	and fold into the mixture.
	Beat again and add:
*3 ½ oz. almonds (100 g)	blanched and ground,
3 tsp cinnamon	
1 tsp cloves	
1 Tbs cardamom	
a dash of white pepper	
*8 Tbs candied lemon peel (80 g)	finely chopped
4 Tbs candied orange peel (40 g)	finely chopped.
	Sift and beat in, two parts of
1 lb + 6 ½ oz. flour (640 g).	Put the remaining flour onto a board, add mixture and knead to a smooth dough. Let rest for at least 1 hour until dough is firm.

Roll out about 1/2" thick. Press into wooden molds or cut out rounds 1 - 1 ½ " in Ø.
Let dry on waxed cookie sheet overnight at room temperature.
Bake a few test-cookies. They should have a soft base and a light top. Otherwise, they are too dry and the bottom must be moistened.
Pfeffernüsse taste best 2 weeks after baking. They can be stored several weeks. Store first uncovered in kitchen.

Bake on center rack	Temperature 300°F (140°C)	Baking time about 20 min.	Store in tin

Elise's Lebkuchen

Beat in a large bowl over - not in - hot water or in a double-boiler until light and fluffy:

9 oz. sugar (250 g)
3 whole eggs.
1 Tbs cinnamon
½ tsp cloves
1 unsprayed lemon

Mixture should be only lukewarm. Add:

the grated rind of

*7 Tbs candied lemon peel (70 g)   finely chopped
*7 Tbs candied orange peel (70 g)   finely chopped

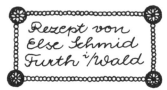

Rezept von Else Schmid Furth i/Wald

*7 oz. hazelnuts (200 g) or
*7 oz. almonds (200 g)
*2 oz. almonds (50 g)

unblanched and ground, and
blanched and coarsely chopped.
Add egg mixture and fold in until evenly blended. If the batter is too soft (because the eggs were very large) allow dough to rest a little longer. Spread dough ½ " high in the center, flattening to the rim on

round oblaten 3 1/2" in Ø.

*candied lemon peel
*almonds.

Elise's Lebkuchen can be glazed with icing. In this case garnish Lebkuchen lovingly b e f o r e baking with a little round piece and stripes of
and blanched and halved
(You can see them through the transparent glaze). Otherwise, you can cover them a f t e r baking with chocolate icing p. 114. In this case decorate the icing while still moist either with

*almonds or
colored sugar.

Bake Elise's Lebkuchen at low heat. If you have a gas oven leave door slightly ajar. This Lebkuchen should be pliable on the oblaten side after baking, else they will be come dry and hard very soon.
(Photo opposite page).

Bake in upper third	Temperature 280-300°F (140-150°C)	Baking time 20 min.	Store in tin in freezing bag

Icing for Elise's Lebkuchen

White icing.

Sift
1 1/2 c. conf. sugar (200 g)   add while stirring
1—2 Tbs hot water   and
2 Tbs arrack.   Continue stirring until icing is glossy:

Pink icing:

Prepare icing as above, but add a few drops of
red food coloring or
red beet juice.

Chocolate icing:

Break
7 oz. unsweetened chocolate (200 g) into pieces and add
3 Tbs hot water.   Melt in double boiler over moderate heat.
                                 Add
1 oz. coconut butter (Palmin) (30 g) stir until smooth. Ice Lebkuchen at once.

Photo overleaf:

        Elise's Lebkuchen, White Lebkuchen
Brownies
        Mock Bread'n Butter

Chocolate Lebkuchen

4 egg whites.
11 ½ oz. sugar (320 g)
*4 ½ oz. almonds (120 g)
*2 ½ oz. semisweet chocolate
     (60 g)
round oblaten

7 oz. semisweet chocolate (200 g).
a nut-sized piece of
coconut butter.

*almonds.

Whip until stiff:
Add and continue beating with
until mixture is thick. Fold in:
unblanched and ground, and

grated. Spread 1/2 - 3/4" thick on
and bake slowly. When slightly cooled,
coat with chocolate icing.
Break into pieces and melt in a double-boiler,
Stir constantly and add

Blend well and ice Lebkuchen immediately.
Garnish with blanched
Dry in a draft-free place.

Bake on center rack	Temperature 320°F (160°C)	Baking time 12-15 min.	Store in tin

White Lebkuchen

6 whole eggs
1 lb + 2 oz. sugar (500 g)
*3 ½ oz. almonds (100 g)
*2 Tbs almonds
*3 ½ oz. candied lemon peel
     (100 g)
1 Tbs cinnamon
1 tsp cloves
a dash of cardamom.
1 lb + 2 oz. flour (500 g)

oblaten 2 x 4"
candied lemon peel

Beat until light and foamy:

unblanched and ground,
blanched and coarsely chopped

finely chopped. Season with

Sift
adding one cup at a time, beating slowly until
well mixed. Spread dough 1/2" thick on oblong
and flatten edges. Press an oblong piece of
into the center. Let dry overnight and bake
until quite light. Store at first uncovered.

Bake on center rack	Temperature 320°F (160°C)	Baking time 15 min.	Store in freezing bag

Brown Cakes

Mix and bring to a boil:

9 oz. light molasses (250 g)
9 oz. dark molasses syrup (250 g)
9 oz. sugar (250 g)
9 oz. lard (250 g).

Let cool slightly.
Sift onto a board:

2,2 lb flour (1000 g)
2 Tbs cinnamon
1 Tbs cloves   and
1 Tbs cardamom.   Add
2 ½ Tbs potash (25 g)   dissolved in
2 Tbs rosewater
*4 ½ oz. almonds (125 g)   unblanched and ground,
*4 ½ oz. candied lemon peel
  (125 g)   minced or finely chopped. Knead well.

Let dough rest for 8 days to four weeks. This means you can bake any quantity you want, any time you want. Roll out dough very thinly, (1/8"), cut into squares with knife or various cookie cutters. You may brush the center of the cakes with some egg whites and dot each with a blanched, halved almond. Bake on well buttered cookie sheet. Remove immediately with a thin knife or cakes will break.

Bake in upper third of oven	Temperature 390°F (200°C)	Baking time 8-10 min.	Store in tin

OLD
FAMILY RECIPE
STOLTENBERG–LERCHE
HAMBURG

Artificial Honey Bars

1 lb + 2 oz. artificial honey
   (500 g).
3 ½ oz. butter (100 g) or
3 ½ oz. margarine (100 g)
1 whole egg
1 unsprayed lemon
4 Tbs sugar
1 Tbs cinnamon
1 tsp cloves
a pinch of cardamom
a pinch of mace
*5 Tbs candied lemon peel (50 g)
*5 Tbs candied orange peel (50 g)
*2 oz. hazelnuts (50 g)

1 lb + 2 oz. flour (500 g)
1 Tbs baking soda.

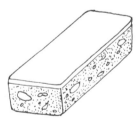

7 oz. conf. sugar (200 g)
2 Tbs arrack or
2 Tbs lemon juice
1 Tbs hot water.

Melt at low heat:

Let cool briefly. Mix with

the finely grated rind of

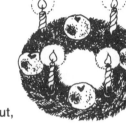

and
both superfinely cut,
coarsely chopped.
Sift together and beat in lightly until well
mixed:

Spread dough (about 2 ¾ " high) into a well
buttered baking pan or large oven-proof pan,
smooth with a spatula and bake in preheated
oven. Do not open while baking. Allow to
cool for 5 minutes, cover with arrack or
lemon glaze and cut into bars 1 x 2" while
still warm. Bars are soft. They can be served
right away. Suitable for St. Nikolaus Day
(6th December) platters and the Advent
Season. For icing, sift:
and add

and
Beat well until icing is thick and glossy.

Bake on center rack	Temperature 350°F (180°C)	Baking time 30 min.	Store in freezing bag

Basler Leckerli

Melt and dissolve:

1 lb + 2 oz. honey (500 g)
7 oz. sugar (200 g).

Add:

2 Tbs cinnamon (20 g)
1 Tbs cloves (10 g)
1 tsp nutmeg

finely ground,
the grated rind of

1 unsprayed lemon.
*7 Tbs candied lemon peel (70 g)
*7 Tbs candied orange peel (70 g)
*8 oz. almonds (230 g)

Stir in

both finely chopped and
shaved.
Sift onto a plain surface:

1 ½ lb flour (700 g).
1 ½ Tbs potash (15 g)
3 Tbs kirsch

Add
dissolved in
and mix all ingredients well to a smooth
dough. Let it rest covered at room
temperature for at least one day.
Then roll out 1/2" thick, place the dough on
a buttered cookie sheet, dusted with flour.
Do not overbake. After baking while still
warm, cover with icing and cut into small
oblongs. For icing, sift:

10 ½ oz. conf. sugar (300 g).
3 Tbs kirsch
3 Tbs hot water

Add

and mix well until glossy. Let rest for some
days uncovered in kitchen before storing.

Bake on center rack	Temperature 350°F (180°C)	Baking time 15 min.	Store in tin

Magenbrot

3 oz. softened butter (80 g)
1 whole egg
13 ½ oz. sugar (375 g)
3 oz. cocoa (80 g).
½ tsp allspice
1 Tbs cinnamon
1 tsp cardamom
1 tsp cloves
*1/2 cup strong coffee.

1 lb + 11 ½ oz. flour (780 g)
2 Tbs baking powder.

9 oz. conf. sugar (250 g)
3 ½ oz. dark cocoa (90 g).
½ cup water

1 Tbs butter

Cream until very foamy:

Sift together and blend in, one cup at a time:

Knead well by hand on a pastry board until
dough is smooth and shiny. Shape rolls
1 ¼ " and flatten sligthly (s. illustration).
Bake on buttered cookie sheet.
(Do not overbake). While still hot, slice obli-
quely. Let cool, then dip into cocoa icing.
For the icing, sift together:

Bring to a boil with
until the mixture draws a thread between two
fingers. Stir in
and apply icing at once.

Bake on center rack	Temperature	Baking time	Store in
Bake on center rack	390°F (200°C)	20-30 min.	tin

Aachener Printen

1 lb dark molasses (450 g)
  (beet syrup)

From

take 3 Tbs, cover and put aside.
Melt remaining molasses with

3 ½ oz. brown sugar (100 g)
3 ½ oz. brown rock candy
  (100 g)

and beat over low heat until sugar has
dissolved. Let cool until luke-warm.
Add:

the spices: 2 Tbs cinnamon, 1 tsp cloves, 2 tsp aniseed, and then ½ tsp from
each: cardamom, allspice, ginger, coriander, and a pinch of salt

1 lb + 3 ½ oz. flour (600 g)
1 ½ Tbs potash (15 g)
3 Tbs rosewater or
3 Tbs arrack

Sift onto a board:
and stir syrup into the middle. Dissolve
in:

and knead to a firm dough. If dough should
be too firm, add some

milk or water.

*3 Tbs candied orange peel (80 g)
*1 unsprayed orange.

Finally, blend in
finely chopped and the shredded rind of
Put dough into a freezing bag, allow to rest at
room temperature for at least 5 days. Then
roll out one piece at a time 1/5" thick and cut
into oblongs 1 x 3". Place on wax paper or
on the rough side of

oblaten

and let rest overnight. Do not overbake. Mix
the reserved
with

3 Tbs syrup
2 Tbs hot water

and stir until combined. Spread hot printen
with mixture for a nice gloss. Store uncovered at first then in a closed tin.
(Photo p. 103)

Bake on center rack	Temperature 350°F (180°C)	Baking time 18 min.	Store in tin

120

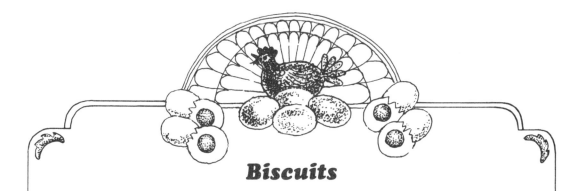

Biscuits

Badener Chräbeli

Beat until very light and foamy:

3 whole eggs
10 ½ oz. conf. sugar (300 g)
1 pinch of salt
1 tsp kirsch
1 tsp aniseed, crushed.

10 ½ oz. flour (300 g).

Sift onto a wooden board:
Fold in the creamed mixture and knead well. If the eggs are larger, add some more flour.
Let rest at least for one hour. Form rolls the thickness of a finger. Cut off sticks 2" long, shape crescents, score in three times. (See illustration).
Place on buttered cookie sheet. Allow surface to dry for 1-2 days. If bottom-side should be too dry, moisten with some water before baking. The Chräbeli should have a soft »base« and the surface should be light. If you bake in gas oven, leave door slightly ajar. Store uncovered at first. For fine flavor, you may sprinkle the bottom of the biscuit-tin with aniseed.

Bake on bottom shelf	Temperature 320°F (160°C)	Baking time 20 min.	Store in tin

Milk Springerle

Most important ingredients: a lot of love and patience.
A tip: do not make springerle when the humidity is high.

Sift into a bowl:

1 ½ lb + 7 oz. warmed flour (875 g)
1 lb + 6 oz. conf. sugar (625 g). Add
1 tsp hartshorn salt (6 g) dissolved in
1 cup lukewarm milk. Blend first with flour-sugar mixture, then knead on a board until smooth. Depending on the kind of flour used the dough may be too stiff. If so, add some milk, or if the dough is too moist, knead in some sifted flour. Wrap in a moist cloth and let rest at least for 1 hour. Divide into parts and roll out to uniform thickness of 1/2". Dust surface with sifted

cornstarch and wrap in smoothly. Press springerle molds into the dough. You may turn the mold over and press the dough in with your fingertips. Do not flour the molds (the flour would clog the fine contoures).

Dough should not be sticky. If you like springerle for decoration, perforate for hanging up. Let dry for several hours on waxed cookie sheet.Drying time is shorter than for Springerle from Aunt Fanny. The surface should remain white while baking. Therefore, place an empty cookie sheet on top shelf. Bake a test cookie. If it has no soft base, it may be overdried. If so, moisten bottom side with some water. If you bake in a gas oven, leave oven door ajar. Cool on wire rack, paint with water colors or distempers. Only if these »pieces of art« are for eating, should food colors be used. If springerle are not perforated, glue a picture hook on the back. Store carefully, break-proof. (Photo opposite page.)

Bake on 2nd shelf from bottom	Temperature 280°F (140°C)	Baking time 30 min.	Store in biscuit tin

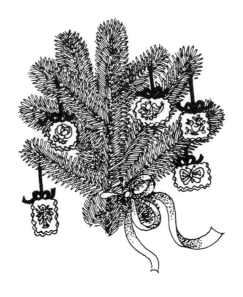

Photo:
Springerle

Springerle (from Aunt Fanny)

Also called »Nürnberger Marzipan«
An old family recipe.

Bake in time (at least two weeks in advance for aging and best flavor!)

Beat

1 lb + 2 oz. sugar (500 g) and
4 egg yolks until combined. Whip
3 egg whites until very stiff, add the shredded rind of
1 unsprayed lemon, fold in the egg yolk mixture and continue stirring in one direction for 45 min. (You may use an electric mixer, but dough will be firmer if stirred manually.) Sift and add:

1 lb + 2 oz. warmed flour (500g). Dissolve
1 tsp potash in
1 Tbs kirsch. Knead all ingredients to a smooth dough and leave wrapped in a moist cloth for a least 1 hour. Pinch off portions and roll them evenly to the dimension of your mold 1/2" thick. Repeated kneading of dough scraps makes springerle dough hard.

Dust with sifted

cornstarch. Rub smooth with the ball of your hand. Press mold into the dough. If you are using larger molds, turn them over and pat dough in lightly with your finger tips. Cut off excess dough with a knife or a jagging wheel at the edges. Let rest in a warm room for at least 24 hours allowing the surface to dry. Bake a test springerle on a buttered or waxed cookie sheet first. The surface should be white and the »base« slightly yellow. When baking in a gas oven, insert a second empty sheet on top shelf. Leave oven door lightly ajar ten minutes after baking. If no »base« has developed, the bottom side has dried out too much. In this case brush bottom with some water. After baking, cover springerle with a dry cloth before storing in a cool place. (Photo p. 83)

Bake on 2nd shelf from bottom	Temperature 265°F (140°C)	Baking time 25-30 min.	Store in tin box

Water Springerle

Salt dough.

Sift onto a wooden board:

1 lb + 2 oz. flour (500 g).   Add

7 oz. superfine salt (200 g),   making a hollow into the center.

Mix well with

1 cup of lukewarm water.   Add:

1 tsp hartshorn salt (5 g)   dissolved in

2 Tbs cold water.   Knead dough well, wrap in foil and let rest for 1-2 hours. Roll out evenly to thickness of 1/3". Dust lightly with sifted

cornstarch   and rub slightly on surface. Press dough into molds by portions and proceed as called for in recipe for Milk-Springerle (page 122). Water springerle may also be dried without baking. In this case, hartshorn salt is not required. As these Springerle can break easily, store them wrapped in tissue paper.

Tip: Rub wooden molds with oil before storing them.
Wipe off excess oil.

Baumkuchen Wedges

7 oz. softened butter (200 g).

Blend until smooth:

7 oz. conf. sugar (200 g)
9 egg yolks
2 Tbs sweet heavy cream
1 Tbs rum.

Sift and add:
and add
one at a time. Combine with

Cream until light and fluffy.
Season finely with the seeds of

1 vanilla bean
½ tsp mace.
9 egg whites.
7 oz. sifted flour (200 g).

and
Whip until stiff:
Fold in loosely with

Butter a small baking tin or a heat-resistant
oblong glass pan generously. Fill batter in thinly
to just cover the bottom. Bake until light.
Add more batter, place rack on top shelf,
bake until light brown. Continue in this manner
until batter is used up. If necessary, place an
empty baking sheet on bottom shelf to prevent
the lower layer from becoming too dark.
Heat and blend until smooth

½ glass apricot jam.

Spread onto the warm cake. Divide baumkuchen
and place onto a wooden board. Cut into little
bars 1 ½ " wide. Cut bars into triangles. When
cooled, coat with melted

chocolate coating
(about 2 cups). p. 114.

Wedges stay fresh a long time.

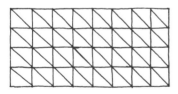

Bake 1 st layer in center 2 nd to last layer on top shelf	Temperature 380°F (250°C)	Baking time 6 min. each	Store ins glass jars

Aniseed Loaves I

3 whole eggs (about 2 oz. each)
   (60 g),
7 oz. superfine sugar (200 g).

Beat until fluffy in a double-boiler:

with

Mixture should be lukewarm, let cool,
continue beating until mixture has a thick,
white creamy consistency.

Sift warmed

*8-9 oz. wheat flour (220-250 g).
*1 tsp aniseed

Fold in 3 Tbs at a time. Finally add
crushed. With two teaspoons drop small
round loaves on waxed and floured cookie
sheets, or use pastry bag with round tip. Let drops dry at room temperature
overnight until tops become dull. Insert a second empty cookie sheet in preheated oven on top shelf so that the surface of the loaves stays nice and white.
The soft cookie base should be light yellow.

Bake on center rack	Temperature 300°F (150°C)	Baking time 12-15 min.	Store in tin

Small Aniseed Zwieback

5 egg whites.

Whip until stiff:
Beat until very creamy and
fold in:

5 egg yolks
7 oz. sugar (200 g).
1 Tbs aniseed
9 oz. flour (250 g).

Add

crushed. Sift and add
Butter a roasting pan or flat baking pan generously. Fill in batter 1" high, bake until golden
yellow and invert pan onto a board. After
cooling cut into strips about 2 ½ " long and
1/2" wide. Next day, place strips sliced side
down, on foil lined cookie sheet and bake at
moderate heat until light yellow.

Bake in upper third of oven	Temperature 340°F (170°C)	Baking time 25 min.	Store in biscuit tin

Biscuits

2 egg yolks
2 Tbs warm water
3 oz. sugar (80 g).

Cream in
a bowl:

Rezept
v.
Omi Edenharter
geb. Fries

2 egg whites
1 tsp lemon juice
1 tsp vanilla extract

Beat in a sepa-
rate mixing bowl:

and
until stiff. Combine with the egg yolk mixture.
Sift together and fold in loosely:

2 ½ oz. - 1 Tbs flour (75 g)
2 oz. cornstarch
(50 g).

On a well buttered cookie sheet dusted with flour
drop (with teaspoon) small heaps 3/4" well apart.
After baking you may decorate cookies with white
icing or melted chocolate.
For icing, whip until stiff

2 Tbs egg white.
4 ½ oz. conf. sugar (125 g)
1 tsp lemon juice

Sift and add:

and beat to a thick consistency. You may tint icing
with

food coloring.

Fill into little parchment bags and draw designs
onto the cookies.

Bake on center rack	Temperature 320°F (160°C)	Baking time 10-15 min.	Store in tin

Wibele

2 whole eggs
4 ½ oz. sugar (130 g)
½ tsp vanilla extract
a dash of cinnamon.
5 oz. flour (140 g).

Whip until light and foamy in a double-boiler:

and
Sift and fold in lightly
On a greased or waxed cookie sheet dusted with
flour place 1-2" Wibele drop by drop with a small
tip of a pastry bag. Allow to dry until tops are quite
dull. (About 3 hours). Then bake until light on tops.
Wibele should have golden yellow »feets«.

Bake on center rack	Temperature 320°F (160°C)	Baking time 10 min.	Store in freezing bags

Candied Orange Peel Loaves

3 whole eggs
9 oz. sugar (250 g)
1 unsprayed lemon
*1 Tbs candied lemon peel
*1 Tbs candied orange peel
1 Tbs orange spirit.*

13 ½ oz. flour (375 g)
1 dash of salt
1 tsp baking soda.

sugar crystals

candied orange peel.

5 ½ oz. conf. sugar (150 g)
2-3 Tbs warm orange juice.

Beat:
with
until creamy. Add the grated rind of

both very finely chopped

Sift together and add:

Knead to a smooth dough. Shape small loaves into the size of your little finger, roll loaves in and bake until yellow or coat after baking with orange glaze and sprinkle with chopped
For glaze, sift and blend until glossy:

Bake on center rack	Temperature 300-350°F (150-180°C)	Baking time 10 min.	Store in freezing bags

Cat's Tongues

3 egg whites
3 Tbs sugar
½ vanilla extract
3 oz. sugar (80 g).
4 ½ oz. flour (125 g)
½ cup heavy cream

Whip until stiff

and another
Into this mixture, carefully sift
and fold in. Add
whipped very stiff. Fill into pastry bag (affixed with round tip). On a waxed cookie sheet, drop 3-4" long tongues. Dot-dash-dot. Place well apart. Mixture melts down during baking!
Bake in preheated oven until set and edges are golden brown.

Bake on center rack	Temperature 300°F (150°C)	Baking time 10-15 min.	Store in biscuit tin

Aniseed Loaves II

	Beat
2 whole eggs.	Then add
7 oz. sugar (200 g)	
1 Tbs vanilla sugar.*	Beat until the mixture is thick and creamy.
	Sift together in a separate bowl
3 ½ oz. wheat flour (100 g)	
3 ½ oz. cornstarch (100 g)	
1 Tbs aniseed (12 g)	crushed. Gradually blend into egg mixture.
	If batter is too soft (because larger eggs were
	used), add some more flour. Place small heaps

of batter (1/2 tsp) on buttered and floured cookie sheet. Let rest at room temperature for 1-2 days until the surface is well dried und dull. Bake. Even after baking, the tops should be meringuelike, the bottoms should have soft golden yellow »feet«. Do not bake if humidity is high!

Bake on center rack	Temperature 300°F (150°C)	Baking time 10-15 min.	Store in biscuit tin.

Almond Thaler

	Melt
1 ½ oz. butter (40 g).	Allow time for cooling.
	In a separate bowl beat until fluffy:
2 egg yolks	
3 ½ oz. sugar (100 g)	
2 drops of bitter almond oil.	Add cooled butter. Blend well.
	In a mixer bowl whip until very stiff:
2 egg whites	
1 Tbs sugar	
1 dash of salt.	Sift together and fold in with whipped egg
	whites
3 ½ oz. flour (100 g)	
1 oz. cornstarch (30 g)	Drop the batter with a teaspoon (spaced well
	apart) on buttered cookie sheet sprinkled with
*blanched and shaved almonds.	Sprinkle cookies likewise on top with
*blanched and shaved almonds.	Bake until set and only edges are brown.

Bake on center rack	Temperature 300°F (150°C)	Baking time 8 min.	Store in tin

Bitter Orange Loaves

4 whole eggs
12 oz. sugar (340 g).
1 unsprayed orange
1 unsprayed lemon.

Beat until very foamy

Add the finely shredded or coarsely grated rind of
and the finely grated rind of

14 oz. flour (400 g)

Sift onto a board:
add the creamed egg mixture and work everything
to a smooth dough.
Knead in

*3 ½ oz. candied orange peel
   (100 g)
*1 ½ oz. candied lemon peel
   (40 g).

Allow dough to rest for one hour at room temperature. Shape a roll as thick as a finger, cut off 2"
slices and shape again. Cut gashes (see illustration) and brush with

2 egg yolks.
*candied orange peel.

Into gashes insert small strips of
Put on buttered and floured cookie sheet.
Bake until golden.

Bake on center rack	Temperature 320°F (160°C)	Baking time 12 min.	Store in tin

Nut Cookies without Shortening

Berlin Bread

Whip
3 (small) whole eggs.	Continue beating while adding (1/2 cup at a time)
7 oz. cane sugar (200 g)	until mixture is light and creamy. Add:
3 oz. apple syrup (80 g) or light molasses	
2 Tbs corn brandy	and the following spices:
2 Tbs cinnamon	
1 pinch of cloves	
1 pinch of allspice.	
	Fold in:
*3 ½ oz. almonds (100 g)	unblanched and coarsely chopped,
*1 ½ oz. candied lemon peel (40 g)	finely chopped,
*3 ½ oz. hazelnuts (100 g)	ground
*3 ½ oz. chocolate (100 g)	grated. Melt and add after cooling
1 ½ oz. butter (40 g).	Sift together and add
5 ½ oz. flour (150 g)	
1 tsp baking soda	and stir until well combined.

Spread mixture 1/2" thick on buttered foil.
Do not overbake! Glaze while still warm.
Cut into 1 x 2" bars.
For the glaze: Sift into a small bowl:

7 oz. conf. sugar 200 g	
1 Tbs lemon juice	
1 Tbs rum	
1 Tbs hot water.	Beat well until glaze is smooth and glossy.

Bake on center rack	Temperature 350-375°F (190-200°C)	Baking time 20 min.	Store in tin

Amaretti

Which don't become hard so quickly.
Mix in a bowl until well combined:

*7 oz. sweet almonds (200 g)
*6 bitter almonds   blanched and ground
2 oz. almond paste (50 g)
5 ½ oz. superfine sugar (160 g).

Whip in another small bowl

2 egg whites
1 dash of salt
2 Tbs sugar   until they hold soft peaks. Fold loosely into
the almond mixture until well mixed. Shape
balls 1 ½ " in Ø and place on non-stick baking
paper. Brush with
rosewater   and dust with
conf. sugar.   If you bake in gas oven, leave door ajar if
needed. Amaretti must be soft inside when
removed from cookie sheet, otherwise they
become hard very quickly. Amaretti taste best
when quite fresh.

Bake on center rack	Temperature 320°F (160°C)	Baking time 30 min.	Store in freezing bag in tin

Geneva Almond Macaroons

In a large bowl, beat over - not in - hot water
until foamy:

7 egg whites
1 tsp lemon juice
1 lb + 2 oz. sugar (500 g)   (one cup at a time)
3 Tbs orange blossom water.   Fold in
1 lb + 2 oz. almonds (500 g)   blanched and finely ground. Mix carefully.
With a wet teaspoon, drop macaroons on
round oblaten   and top each with a blanched halved
*almond.   Bake until lightly yellow. If you bake in gas oven,
leave door ajar if needed.

Bake on center rack	Temperature 280°F (140°C)	Baking time 25 min.	Store in tightly closed tin

Widows's Kisses

*9 oz. almonds (250 g)
2 ½ oz. sugar (60 g)

*9 oz. unsweetened chocolate
    (250g)

4 egg whites
9 oz. sugar (250 g).

oblaten

Put onto a cookie sheet:
blanched and slivered. Sprinkle with
und roast in oven until light yellow.
While still hot, mix with
grated.Break mixture apart with a fork and let
cool.
In a bowl beat over hot water

Fold in the chocolate-almonds.
Drop little heaps on the rough side of split
and bake slowly. If you bake in gas oven,
leave door ajar if needed.

Bake on center rack	Temperature 300°F (140°C)	Baking time 15-20 min.	Store in tin freezing bags

Japs

7 egg whites
8 ½ oz. sugar (240 g)
2 Tbs vanilla sugar*.
*8 ½ oz. hazelnuts (240 g)
2 oz. flour (50 g).

5 ½ oz. softened butter (150 g)
4 oz. conf. sugar (120 g).
*5 ½ oz. unsweetened chocolate
    (150 g)

Whip until foamy:

Fold in
slightly roasted, finely ground,

With teaspoon or pastry bag place drops of
1 ½ " (spaced well apart) on a well buttered
and floured cookie sheet. Bake until only the
edges are brown. Meanwhile prepare filling.
Cream:

Stir in

very finely grated. When the japs are cool
spread bottoms with ½ tsp of cream and
put 2 cookies together.

Bake on center rack	Temperature 300-350°F (150-175°C)	Baking time 8-10 min.	Store in airtight tin

Coconut Macaroons

Stir over low heat in
a heat-resistant saucepan:

4 egg whites
7 oz. sugar (200 g)
1 Tbs honey
5 ½ oz. grated coconut (150 g)

until all ingredients are well combined.
Remove from heat. Sift and fold into the warm
mixture:

2 oz. flour (50 g)
1 unsprayed lemon.
oblaten

and the shredded rind of
With a teaspoon place nut-sized heaps on
and bake until macaroons are firm to the touch
but moist inside. Remove from cookie sheet
while still hot.

Bake on center rack	Temperature 280°F (140°C)	Baking time 20 min.	Store in freezing bags

Coconut Moors

Beat over - not in - hot water until stiff:

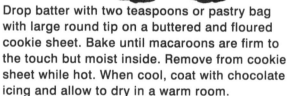

3 egg whites
6 ½ oz. sugar (180 g)
1 Tbs lemon juice.
8 ½ oz. grated coconut (240 g).

Fold in
Drop batter with two teaspoons or pastry bag
with large round tip on a buttered and floured
cookie sheet. Bake until macaroons are firm to
the touch but moist inside. Remove from cookie
sheet while hot. When cool, coat with chocolate
icing and allow to dry in a warm room.
For icing, melt in double-boiler:

6 ½ oz. unsweetened chocolate
(180 g)
1 Tbs butter.
6 Tbs water
5 Tbs sugar.

In another pan boil for 2-3 min.

Then stir slowly into the chocolate-butter
mixture. Remove from heat, stir until thick
and lukewarm.

Bake on center rack	Temperature 280°F (140°C)	Baking time 20 min.	Store in glass jars

Vanilla Chocolate Fingers

In a saucepan, over low heat, combine:

*12 ½ oz. almonds (350 g)
7 oz. sugar (200 g)
vanilla bean
1/3 cup orange blossom water
1/3 cup water.

blanched and ground the seeds of a whole

von
Gertrude
Hubert
1864

*3 ½ oz. semisweet chocolate (100 g)

Stir to a fine dough having a smooth consistency. Fold into the warm mixture finely ground. Spread the mixture 1" thick onto the working surface (moistened with water). Cut off sticks the size of your little finger and roll them in

*about 7 oz. almonds (200 g)

blanched and shaved.
Place on well buttered foil or sheet. Allow to dry briefly. Bake slowly. Should be slightly moist inside. Do not store too long.

Bake on center rack	Temperature 320°F (160°C)	Baking time 20-25 min.	Store in glass jars

Genuine Almond Macaroons

Combine and put twice through a grinder

*8 oz. almonds (230 g)
6 ½ oz. sugar (180 g).
½ lemon
1 egg white

blanched and ground
Add the juice of

and beat the mixture in a saucepan over low heat until lukewarm. Set aside. Meanwhile whip until foamy:

3 egg whites
2 oz. sugar (50 g)

and mix carefully with the almond paste. Place drops 1" in Ø on

oblaten,
*almonds.

and garnish with halved, blanched
Let dry slightly, bake until set.

Bake on center rack	Temperature 280°F (140°C)	Baking time 20 min.	Store in freezing bags

Wasp's Nests

Mela Michel

9 oz. sugar (250 g)
4 Tbs water

Heat:

until sugar is completely dissolved.
Add

*9 oz. almonds (250 g)

unblanched, slivered and roast until lightly
brown - stirring constantly. Remove from heat
and stir occasionally to prevent sticking
together. Beat over - not in - hot water:

6 egg whites
9 oz. sugar (250 g)

until mixture is thick and foamy. Add

*4 ½ oz. semisweet
   chocolate (125 g)
½ vanilla bean

grated, the seeds scraped out from
and the cooled almonds. With a teaspoon place
drops on

round oblaten.

Bake slowly. If you bake in gas oven, leave door
ajar if necessary.

Bake on center rack	Temperature 280°F (140°C)	Baking time 20 min.	Store in tin

Chocolate Shells

Whip until they stand in stiff peaks:

8 egg whites.
1 lb + 2 oz. sugar (500 g)

Add
and beat to a thick foam.
Add juice and grated rind of

1 unsprayed lemon.
*6 ½ oz. chocolate (180 g)
1 Tbs cinnamon
*1 lb + 2 oz. almonds (500 g)

Stir in
grated, and

aus Omas Schul-Kochbuch 1891

unblanched and ground. Shape balls, press into
shell-shaped molds dredged with
Unmold, chill. Bake slowly.

sugar.

Bake on center rack	Temperature 265 °F (130°C)	Baking time 12 min.	Store in tin

Zimmetsterne

4 egg whites
11 oz. sugar (310 g).

Beat over - not in - hot water until foamy:

Set aside ½ cup of this mixture. Stir into the remainder the juice and the grated rind of

1 unsprayed lemon
1 tsp cinnamon.
*9 oz. almonds (250 g)

Fold in
unblanched and ground. Divide into fist-sized portions, roll 1/2" thick onto a pastry board sprinkled with

*chopped almonds.

Cut out medium sized stars (dipping cutter repeatedly in water) and place on the rough side of split

oblaten.

Ice the tops with the reserved mixture using a pastry bag. Bake carefully. Insert second baking sheet on top shelf, icing should remain light. Bottom of stars must yield to pressure after baking or they will become dry. Let stand uncovered before storing.

Bake on center rack	Temperature 240-280°F (120-140°C)	Baking time 20-30 min.	Store in freezing bags

Choco-Walnut-Squares

4 egg yolks
4 ½ oz. sugar (120 g).
*5 oz. chocolate (140 g)
*5 oz. walnuts (140 g)
2 Tbs bread crumbs.

Beat until very foamy:

Melt in double-boiler and stir in:

ground, and
Combine all ingredients to a dough. Spread dough on a well buttered cookie sheet or place batter 1/2" thick in an ovenproof pan. Ice after baking. Let cool slightly. Cut into small squares or oblongs with a sharp knife. For icing, mix:

Rezepte von G. Sonnleitner

5 ½ oz. conf. sugar (150 g)
1 Tbs lemon juice
2 Tbs hot water.

Blend well and use at once.

Bake on center rack	Temperature 360-375°F (190-200°C)	Baking time 20 min.	Store in tin

141

Munich Cinnamon Stars

5 ½ oz. hazelnuts (150 g)
5 ½ oz. almonds (150 g)
9 oz. sugar (250 g)
*4 ½ oz. almond paste (125 g)
*7 ½ Tbs candied orange peel (75 g)
*7 ½ Tbs candied lemon peel (75 g)
1 Tbs cinnamon (12 g)
1 dash of salt
1 unsprayed lemon.
4 unbeaten egg whites.

Combine onto a board:

both unblanched and ground

cut into small pieces,

both finely chopped,

and the grated rind of
Add and mix with
Let dough rest for 2 days.
Roll out dough 1/6" thick. Cut out small
stars, ice and bake slowly. Stars should not
be too dry. For icing beat:

3 egg whites

until they form stiff peaks. Beat in (1/2 cup
at a time)

1 lb conf. sugar (450 g)

sifted, until mixture stands in peaks ready
to spread. For an exciting taste fold in

1 pinch of orange peel

superfinely grated. (Photo opposite page).

Bake on center rack	Temperature 300-320°F (150-160°C)	Baking time 10-15 min.	Store in tin

Lemon Hearts

3 egg yolks
4 ½ oz. sugar (130 g).
1 Tbs lemon juice
1 unsprayed lemon.
*8 oz. almonds
(230 g)

Cream until foamy:

Add
and the grated rind of
Place on a board:
blanched and ground. Add egg mixture and
knead quickly to a smooth dough. Roll out
1/6" thick and cut out hearts 2" in size. Bake
lightly on buttered aluminum foil. Place on
wire rack and coat with lemon icing while still
hot. For icing, stir until smooth:

3 ½ oz. conf. sugar (100 g)
1 Tbs lemon juice.

and

*Rezept v.
Taute Liesel
Graz*

Bake on center rack	Temperature 350°F (180°C)	Baking time 12 min.	Store in biscuit tin

Photo:
Cinnamon Stars

Almond Arches

Beat over - not in - hot water:

3 small egg whites
6 ½ oz. sugar (180 g)
1 tsp lemon juice

(mixture should only be lukewarm).
Fold in

*6 oz. almonds (175 g),
*1 oz. candied lemon peel (30 g)

quite dry and shaved, and
finely chopped. Spread mixture 1/5" thick
on oblong

oblaten.
*almonds.

Sprinkle with shaved
Pat down slightly. With a sharp knife cut off
stripes about 1" wide and 4" long. Let dry for
2 hours, bake until only edges are lightly brown.
While still hot and flexible, place stripes over
rolling pin or bottle. Dip ends into melted

coating chocolate.

Let dry in a warm room.

Bake on center rack	Temperature 350°F (180°C)	Baking time 20 min.	Store in tin

Almond Hearts

Beat until foamy:

3 egg whites
9 oz. sugar (250 g).
1 tsp cinnamon
1 dash of cloves
*2 Tbs candied lemon peel
*9 oz. almonds (250 g)

Add:

finely chopped. Work to a dough with
unblanched and ground. Chill briefly. Roll out
1/6" thick. Cut out medium-sized hearts and
re-chill. Bake on buttered foil.
When cool, cover with

chocolate coating.
*almonds.

Top with blanched, diagonally cut
Let dry well. Store first in cardboard box.

Bake on center rack	Temperature 265°F (130°C)	Baking time 15 min.	Store in tin in freezing bags

Tyrolian Leckerli

Beat until very foamy:

3 whole eggs
4 ½ oz. sugar (130 g)
1 Tbs lemon sugar*.

Sift and stir loosely (1/2 cup at a time)
5 ½ oz. flour (150 g) | into the mixture and add
*3 ½ oz. hazelnuts (100 g) | coarsely chopped,
*3 ½ oz. almonds (100 g)
*3 ½ oz. chocolate (100 g) | also coarsely chopped.
*3 ½ oz. currants or
seedless raisins | soaked in some
Obstler | and
1 tsp cinnamon. | Let batter rest, allowing to
stiffen. Drop small mounds on

round oblaten (1 ½" in Ø). | Note that bottoms of cookies should
yield to pressure after baking. Glaze, top with

½ candied cherry. | For glaze, stir until glossy:
5 ½ oz. conf. sugar (150 g)
2 Tbs lemon juice* | and
2 Tbs hot water.

Bake on center rack	Temperature 350°F (180°C)	Baking time 12 min.	Store in tin in freezing bags

Date Balls

Beat together in a double-boiler:

3 egg whites
5 ½ oz. sugar (150 g).

Blend in
*5 ½ oz. fresh walnuts (150 g) | skinned and coarsely chopped (soak older
nuts in warm milk before removing the skins)
*3 ½ oz. dates (100 g) | pitted and cut into small strips,
1 tsp apricot liquor. | Shape small balls. Place balls on a well
buttered cookie sheet, dusted with
conf. sugar. | Bake slowly.
Let stand uncovered before storing.

Bake on center rack	Temperature 245-280°F (120-140°C)	Baking time 15-20 min.	Store in tin

Hazelnut Macaroons

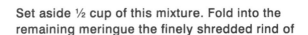

Beat until foamy in a double-boiler

4 egg whites (about 140 g)
8 oz. sugar (230 g)
1 tsp lemon juice.

Set aside ½ cup of this mixture. Fold into the remaining meringue the finely shredded rind of

½ unsprayed lemon
*7 oz. hazelnuts (200 g)

slightly roasted and ground. Dough should be soft. If too soft, let rest for 1 hour or add some more hazelnuts. With 2 teaspoons drop balls on

oblaten (1" in Ø).

With a pastry bag top each macaroon with a small dab of the reserved meringue and crown with

1 whole hazelnut.

(Photo p. 93).

Bake on center rack	Temperature 280°F (140°C)	Baking time 20-30 min.	Store in tin

Hazelnut Diamonds

Beat to a thick cream:

8 egg whites
1 lb + 2 oz. conf. sugar (500 g)

finely sifted and dry.
Set aside one cup of this mixture for icing.
Stir into the remaining mixture the grated rind of

1 unsprayed lemon.
*9 oz. almonds (250 g)
*9 oz. hazelnuts (250 g)

Fold in
unblanched and ground
slightly roasted and ground. Sprinkle working surface with sugar, pinch off small pieces of dough and roll out 1/5" thick. Cut into rhombuses of about 3" with knife or jagging wheel. Place on foil-lined cookie sheet and brush with saved icing. Sprinkle the center with

chopped nuts

and bake carefully. (If oven is too hot icing will crack). Store in cardboard box first.

Bake on center rack	Temperature 280°F (140°C)	Baking time 20 min.	Store in tinbox

Chocolate Rings

	Whip
4 egg whites	until they hold soft peaks
	sift and add:
9 oz. conf. sugar (250 g)	Stir (preferably by hand
	for 15 min.) Fold in:
*9 oz. almonds (250 g)	unblanched and ground,
*3 oz. chocolate (80 g)	finely grated. Fill into pastry bag, and shape
	rings on a well buttered cookie sheet.
	After baking, coat with white icing.
	For the icing, sift
7 oz. conf. sugar (200 g)	add
2 Tbs arrack	
2 Tbs hot water	and stir well until icing is glossy and thick.

Bake on center rack	Temperature 320°F (160°C)	Baking time 20-30 min.	Store in tin

Chocolate Macaroons

	Whip
4 egg whites	and
2 Tbs vanilla sugar*.	until they hold stiff peaks:
	Beat in (1 Tbs at a time)
6 ½ oz. sugar (180 g).	Sift and add
2 ½ oz. dark cocoa (75 g)	
*9 oz. almonds (250 g)	unblanched and ground. With a teaspoon, drop
	small mounds of the batter on
round oblaten (1" in Ø).	Bake slowly.

Bake on center rack	Temperature 280°F (140°C)	Baking time 10-15 min.	Store in freezing bag

Walnut Buns

Whip until stiff:

4 egg whites
1 dash of salt.

9 oz. sugar (250 g)

Slowly beat in
until mixture begins to wriggle.
Add:

*7 oz. walnuts (200 g)
*2 oz. walnuts (50 g)
*2 oz. candied orange peel
(50 g)
round oblaten (1-2")

finely ground
coarsely chopped and

finely chopped. Place balls on small
flatten. Bake until light brown. If you bake in gas
oven, leave door ajar if necessary. Let cool,
spread thinly with

redcurrant jelly
coating chocolate.
*1/2 walnut.

and cover with melted
Top each bun with
(Photo p. 93).

Bake on center rack	Temperature 265°F (130°C)	Baking time 8-10 min.	Store in glass jars

Tuiles Noisette

Beat in double-boiler:

3 egg whites
4 ½ oz. sugar (125 g)
1 Tbs vanilla sugar*.
*4 ½ oz. hazelnuts (125 g)

Blend in
slightly roasted and ground. Form oval
tongues 3" long onto a buttered cookie sheet.
Bake until only edges are light brown.
If you bake in gas oven, leave door ajar if
necessary. While hot, put tongues
over bottles or rolling pin.

Bake on center rack	Temperature 220°F (100°C)	Baking time 8-10 min.	Store in tin in freezing bag

Nut Macaroons

Beat to a thick foam:

4 egg whites
1 tsp lemon juice
9 oz. sugar (250 g)
2 Tbs vanilla sugar*.

Stir until well blended. Set aside ½ cup of this mixture. Fold into the meringue

*4 ½ oz. hazelnuts (125 g)
*4 ½ oz. almonds (125 g)

ground
unblanched, finely chopped. Shape small balls and place on rectangular

oblaten.

Top with the saved up icing. Garnish each cookie with ½ hazelnut. Let rest 1-2 hours. Bake until firm to the touch but not dry. If you bake in gas oven, open door slightly. Break off oblaten along the borders. Leave uncovered before storing.

Bake on center rack	Temperature 265°F (130°C)	Baking time 20 min.	Store in tin

Oat & Nut Kisses

Beat until very fluffy:

3 egg whites
1 Tbs sugar.

well cooled,
Add:

5 oz. sugar (140 g)
1 Tbs vanilla sugar*

and continue beating until mixture has a firm consistency. Roast lightly without shortening:

*3 ½ oz. rolled oats (100 g).
*3 ½ oz. walnuts (100 g)
1 Tbs lemon juice
1 unsprayed lemon.

Let cool. Blend into the meringue:
not too finely ground
and the grated rind of
With 2 teaspoons, drop batter on the rough side of split

rectangular oblaten

and bake. Let cool and leave uncovered for a few days before storing in a closed tin.

Bake on center rack	Temperature 350°F (180°C)	Baking time 10-12 min.	Store in tin

Date Macaroons

Beat until light and foamy:

3 whole eggs
10 ½ oz. sugar (300 g).
10 ½ oz. mixed nuts (300 g)
10 ½ oz. dates (300 g)
2 Tbs vanilla sugar*.
oblaten (1" in Ø)

Fold in:
finely ground
pitted and cut into very fine pieces and
Place mounds on
and bake slowly. When cool, leave uncovered
in kitchen for a few days before storing in an air-
tight container.

Bake on center rack	Temperature 270°F (130-140°C)	Baking time 15-20 min.	Store in tin

Belgrad Bread

Beat together:

6 eggs
1 lb + 2 oz. sugar (500 g)
*1 lb + 2 oz. hazelnuts (500 g)
*3 ½ oz. candied lemon peel
    (100 g)
*3 oz. candied orange peel
    (80 g)
1 unsprayed lemon
1 tsp cinnamon
2 Tbs plum brandy.
13 ½ oz. flour (375 g).

until very frothy, add
ground

Rezept
Justi Reischer
Cham

both diced, the shredded rind of

Sift and blend in:
Depending on size of eggs, let dough rest for
1-2 days at room temperature until firm.
Roll out 1/5" thick and cut into rhombuses with
jagging wheel. Bake on buttered sheet.
Coat while warm with the following glaze.
Sift and stir together:

9 oz. conf. sugar (250 g)
2 Tbs lemon juice
2 Tbs hot water

until glaze is smooth and shiny. Return to oven
for 2 minutes.

Bake on center rack	Temperature 340°F (170°C)	Baking time 15 min.	Store in tin

Meringues *from Rola Vestner*

Important: Use exact amount given in recipe, do not double, paste would stand too long and get firm.

4 very cold egg whites
9 ½ oz. sugar (250 g)
1 tsp lemon juice

In a bowl (set over a saucepan with hot water) beat with

until stiff peaks form. Mixture should be only luke-warm! If you wish, you can add the finely grated rind of

1 unsprayed lemon.

Transfer the meringue mixture to a pastry bag, fitted with a 1/3" decorative tip. Pipe it in small wreaths and rosettes onto greased and floured aluminum foil. Sprinkle with shaved

pistachios
almonds.

or shredded

chocolate icing (p. 114)

Another method: coat meringues with

and sprinkle with

colored sugar.

The meringues are dried out rather than baked. Meringues are done when they are firm and easy to move about on the foil. When cool, store immediately in a tightly sealed container.

Bake on center rack	Temperature 210°F (100°C)	Baking time 30 min.	Store in tin

Meringue Swirls & Baskets

4 very cold egg whites
1/8 tsp cream of tartar
10 ½ oz. sugar (300 g).

Prepare meringue like above:
(best if eggs are a few days old)

You may tint parts of the paste, pink with a few drops of the juice of fresh red beets or red food coloring, or yellow with some saffron. Or decorate meringues with small gold or silver sugar pearls or festive fixings. Photo next page.

Photo:
Meringue Swirls

Luxemburgerli

Whip in a glass bowl:

2 egg whites
1 dash of salt
3 ½ oz. sugar (100 g)
1 Tbs vanilla sugar*

until fluffy.
Sift and add

1 Tbs dark cocoa
(strongly de-oiled)

fill mixture into pastry bag fitted with decorative tip. Place small mounds 1" in Ø on buttered sheet dusted with flour. Bake slow. If you bake in a gas oven, leave door open completely if necessary. The bottoms must yield lightly to the touch. When cool, spread bottom sides with ½ tsp. filling and assemble 2 meringues. Store in a very cool and dry place. Since they do not keep well, they should be consumed soon. For the filling, stir:

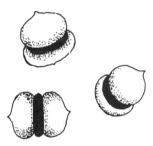

3 oz. butter (80 g)
2 ½ oz. conf. sugar (60 g)
2 small egg yolks.

Melt, let cool and blend in slowly:

2 oz. semisweet chocolate
(50 g).

Bake on bottom rack	Temperature 225°F (140°C)	Baking time 30-40 min.	Store in glass jars for only a brief period

Lemon Meringues

Whip in a
glass bowl:

2 cold egg whites
1 Tbs sugar
1 tsp lemon juice.
4 ½ oz. sugar (125 g)

Add:

Beat until mixture holds stiff peaks. Add the
grated rind of

1 unsprayed lemon.

Fill mixture into pastry bag or place mounds
with 2 teaspoons on a buttered and lightly
floured cookie sheet. Let dry rather than bake.

They are done when they don't yield to the touch and can be moved on the sheet.
If you bake in gas oven, leave door open if necessary. Let cool and store immediately in a sealed tin.

Bake on center rack	Temperature 210°F (100° C)	Baking time 20-30 min.	Store in airtight tin

Meringue Eggs

Pour into a grease-free glass bowl
and beat over - not in - boiling water until mixture
begins to wriggle. Should be lukewarm only!

3 cold egg whites
7 oz. sugar (200 g)
2 Tbs vanilla sugar*.

With 2 wet teaspoons place small eggs on a
buttered and floured cookie
sheet or foil.
Garnish with slivered

*almonds or
colored sugar
(hundreds & thousands)

and let dry at low heat. The almonds should be just
lightly brown. If you bake in gas oven, leave door
open completely if necessary.

Bake on center rake	Temperature 210°F(100°C)	Baking time about 20-30 min.	Store in tin

Rose Hip Meringues

Beat in glass bowl
over - not in - boiling water:

3 egg whites (3 ½ oz.)
7 ½ oz. sugar (210 g)
1 dash of salt

until foamy and thick. The mixture should hold
stiff peaks (allow to become only lukewarm).
Fill ½ cup into a cookie press and chill.
Stir into the remaining mixture

6 ½ oz. raw rose-hip marrow
   (180 g)
1 tsp lemon juice.

Fold in

*7 oz. almonds (200 g)

blanched and ground. With 2 teaspoons place
mounds on small

round oblaten (1" in Ø).

Depress center with the handle of a wet
teaspoon. Fill with

rose-hip jam

and top filling with the reserved meringue paste.
Let dry for ½ hour. Bake slowly at low heat.
Meringues should be slightly soft when removed
from the oven. If you bake in gas oven, leave
door open if necessary. (Photo p. 93)

Bake on center rack	Temperature	Baking time	Store in
center rack	265°F (140°C)	about 40 min.	freezing bag

Date Kisses

Whip until stiff (but not dry):

3 egg whites
1 tsp sugar
1 tsp lemon juice.
3 oz. conf. sugar (80 g).
*3 oz. almonds (80 g)
*5 ½ oz. dates (150 g)

Add and whip again with sifted
Blend in:
blanched and slivered
pitted and cut into small strips. With a teaspoon
place batter on

round oblaten (1" in Ø).

Let dry slowly in oven. If you bake in gas oven,
leave door ajar if necessary.

Bake on center rack	Temperature	Baking time	Store in
center rack	265°F(140°C)	20 min.	tin

Basler Brunsli

*7 oz. almonds (200 g)
7 oz. conf. sugar (200 g)
*4 ½ oz. unsweetened
  chocolate (125 g)
2-3 Tbs. kirsch
1 Tbs water.

fine sugar crystals.

Put onto a board and combine:
unblanched and ground
sifted

grated

Knead by hand to a firm dough. Roll out 1 piece at a time 1/2" thick on
Cut out with cookie cutters if you have no typical mold. Place cookies on a well buttered cookie sheet or foil and dry rather than bake. If you bake in gas oven, leave door ajar if necessary. Tops of Brunsli should not be cracked. When baked, let cool briefly on sheet then place on wire rack. When cooled completely, store immediately since they tend to harden.

Bake on center rack	Temperature 210°F (100°C)	Baking time 5-8 min.	Store in tin

Chocolate Kisses

Whip until stiff:

5 egg whites (about 6 oz.) (165g)
1 tsp lemon juice.
9 oz. sugar (250 g)

*4 ½ oz. almonds (125 g)
*7 oz. semisweet chocolate
  (200 g)

round oblaten (1" in Ø).

Add
and beat until thick and creamy. Set aside and chill 3 Tbs of mixture. Into the remainder, fold in blanched and ground

finely grated. Place with 2 teaspoons small mounds on
Depress center with wet wooden spoon handle. Fill preferably with pastry bag with 1/2" tip. Bake carefully. If you bake in gas oven, keep oven, door ajar if necessary.

Bake on center rack	Temperature 265°F(140°C)	Baking time 30 min.	Store in tin box

Macaroon Bars

	Beat over - not in - boiling water until very foamy:
2 whole eggs	
6 ½ oz. sugar (180 g)	
½ tsp vanilla extract	
1 Tbs orange juice	
5 Tbs candied lemon peel (50 g)	very finely chopped
7 oz. almonds (200 g)	blanched and grated. Transfer the mixture to a pastry bag with a star shaped tip. Pipe stripes onto
oblong oblaten	1" apart. Bake until golden brown. Fill the grooves with pureed hot
apricot jam	and cut into small stripes. (See drawing). Taste best when fresh.

Bake on center rack	Temperature 360°F (180°C)	Baking time 15-20 min.	Store in freezing bag

Orange Macaroons

	Beat in a large bowl:
3 egg whites (3 ½ oz.)	until they hold soft peaks. While beating, add
10 oz. sugar (280 g)	¼ cup at a time. Beat the meringue until it holds stiff peaks. Fold in
*10 oz. almonds (280 g)	blanched and finely ground, the juice and the thinly shredded rind of
1 unsprayed orange.	Split
round oblaten (1" in Ø).	Place, on the split side, mounds of the macaroon mix. Let rest at room temperature overnight. Bake in low oven. Macaroons should be rather dried than baked. The inside should be moist. Place on wire rack and glaze while still hot. For the glaze, sift

7 oz. conf. sugar (200 g).	Add
1 Tbs hot water	
2 Tbs orange spirit*	or
2 Tbs Grand Marnier.	Blend well, folding in the superfinely grated rind of
1 unsprayed orange.	

Bake on center rack	Temperature 250°F (130°C)	Baking time 18-20 min.	Store in freezing bag

Ginger Kisses

Do not prepare if weather is humid!

Beat in a bowl over - not in - boiling water:

4 egg whites
7 oz. brown sugar (200 g)   until foamy.
                                       Fold in:
*2 Tbs candied ginger   cut into fine strips
 1 Tbs orange juice
*1 lb + 2 oz. almonds (500 g)   blanched, slivered and lightly roasted with
 1 ½ oz. sugar (40 g)   and cooled. Drop small amounts of the mixture
                                       with a teaspoon on a buttered and floured
                                       cookie sheet. Garnish each kiss with a little
candied ginger   chip of and bake until light golden. If you use
                                       a gas oven, leave if necessary, the door slightly
                                       open. (Photo p. 73)

Bake on center rack	Temperature 250°F (120°C)	Baking time 20 min.	Store in tin

160

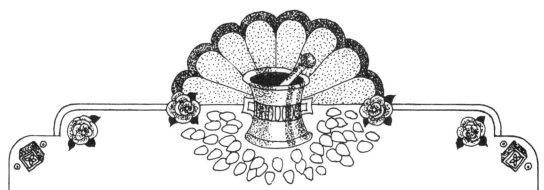

Marzipan and Confections

Marzipan Leckerle

Grind very finely (but do not overdo) by using an electric blender or mixer:

*1 lb + 2 oz. sweet almonds (500 g)

*6 bitter almonds (10 g)

blanched. If possible, mash additionally with a pestle or run twice through meat grinder. Add:

9 oz. superfine sugar (250 g) or
9 oz. conf. sugar (250 g)

2 egg whites

and as much

orange blossom water

as to get a thick, moist paste. Stir over low heat in a heat resistant saucepan until paste comes away from the bottom of the pan.

Dust a cool hard surface with sifted

conf. sugar.

Roll out paste 1/2" thick, press into wooden molds, unmold, or cut out shapes with a cookie cutter and let dry for 2 days. Then bake briefly until lightly brown on top.

Bake on top shelf	Temperature 460°F (250°C)	Baking time 5 min.	Store in glass jar

Königsberger Marzipan

Soak in cold water for about 24 hours:

*1 lb + 2 oz. almonds (500 g)
*6 bitter almonds (18 g).

Remove skins and grind when dry in a
nut grinder. Put almonds in a heat-resistant
saucepan, add

1 lb + 2 oz. conf. sugar
1 Tbs rose water

and knead to a smooth paste. Allow to rest and
keep covered for several days.
(In a heat-resistant pot. Do not use metal saucepan!) Stir paste at very low temperature until it
comes away from the bottom of the pan.

Allow to cool, then re-knead (one piece at a time) and roll out to a thickness of
1/4". Cut out small rounds and hearts. Roll out another oblong of paste four times
as thick, cut off strips 1/2" wide and moisten with rose water. Wrap around edges
of cut out-shapes. Notch the tops, brush with rose water and bake until light
brown. Brush again.

After cooling fill with icing. Combine:

1 lb + 2 oz. conf. sugar (500 g)
1 tsp egg white
1 tsp lemon juice
1 Tbs rosewater.

Stir long and thoroughly. Decorate immediately
with candied fruits. (Photo p. 163)

Bake on top shelf	Temperature 250°F(130°C)	Baking time 8-10 min.	Store in glass jars

Marzipan Mushrooms

Knead well on a hard surface,
like glass or marble:

3 ½ oz. sifted conf. sugar (100 g)
3 ½ oz. almond paste (100g)
1 Tbs rum.
1 tsp cocoa and
1 Tbs hot water

Shape hats and stems. Blend

and brush hats with mixture. Brush bottoms of
stems with

egg white.
pistachios.
egg white

Dip in finely chopped
Glue dry hats and stems together with
Store mushrooms in glass jars.
Do not bake! (Photo p. 163).

Photo:

Several kinds of Marzipan:

Königsberger Marzipan	Marzipan Rolls
Marzipan Mushrooms	Marzipan Potatoes
	Marzipan Carrots

Marzipan Paste I

*9 oz. almonds (250 g)
  3 Tbs bitter almonds (15 g)   are blanched, ground twice and kneaded
                                                 briefly with

  6 ½ oz. conf. sugar (180 g)   and as much
  rosewater   as is required to form a smooth paste.
                                                     This paste is used to shape potatoes and other
                                                     figures - if commercial almond paste is not
                                                     available.

**Fine Marzipan Paste for
Tartlets and Torten:**

Beat 3 small egg whites with 3 ½ ozs. sifted powdered sugar (100 g) over boiling water. Add another 14 ozs. powdered sugar (400 g) (1/2 cup at a time). Blanch, grind and put through meat-grinder 1 lb + 2 ozs. almonds (500 g) and mix thoroughly with the egg whites. Stir these ingredients in a saucepan in boiling water until paste comes away from bottom of pan. When cool, press into molds. Unmold and let dry. (An old recipe).

Marzipan Paste II

                                           Mix
*10 ½ oz. almonds (300 g)   blanched and very finely ground with
  5 ½ oz. conf. sugar (150 g)   and enough
  rosewater   to make a firm moist paste. Stir paste
                                                     in a pan over low heat until it comes away from
                                                     the bottom.
                                                     (Do not use metal pan).
                                                     Sift onto a board:
  3 ½ oz. conf. sugar (100 g)   add paste, knead all briefly and form into
                                                     any desired shape. (Photo p. 83).

Marzipan Lebkuchen

Knead to a smooth dough,
on a surface like glass or marble:

7 oz. almond paste (200 g)
7 oz. conf. sugar (200 g)
1 tsp rosewater or arrack:

Roll out 1/3" thick on

oblong oblaten

and cut into small lebkuchen 2 x 3". Brush with a beaten

egg

and top with halved

*almonds.

Bake until light brown, but not dry.
Glaze while stillwarm. For the glaze, sift

5 ½ oz. conf. sugar (150 g). Beat with
1 Tbs hot water
1 Tbs arrack

to a thin, glossy consistency.

Bake on top shelf	Temperature 340°F(170°C)	Baking time 10-15 min.	Store in glass jars

Marzipan Buns

Knead on a smooth - not wooden - surface:

9 oz. almond paste (250 g)   cut into thin slices,
6 ½ oz. conf. sugar (180 g)   sifted, and
3 tsp rosewater

to a smooth dough. Shape very small loaves,
buns and pretzels 1/2" - 1" long. Brush twice with

egg yolks,

score and bake very briefly on foil or parchment
paper. Do not store too long. Nice for children.
(Photo p. 163).

Bake on top shelf	Temperature 460°F(250°C)	Baking time 4 min.	Store in glass jars

nce upon a time, there was a king who had a very beautiful daughter. Many men wanted her for a wife, but she cared for none of them - they were not to her liking. So she decided to create a man who would please her. She took 18 kilograms of sweet almonds, 17 kilograms of sugar, 17 kilograms of super-fine semolina flour and 5 ladles full of fragrant rosewater. In a slow and toilsome process she crushed the almonds and kneaded them with the sugar, the rosewater and the semolina flour. She then set about shaping a man and when the work was done, sat him upright against the wall of the house where the icons hung. Many a long night she prayed to God that he be brought to life. It was not until the fortieth night that God answered her prayers and brought him to life.

He was very handsome and

beautifully shaped and they named him **Prince Marzipan.**

His name became famous all over the world ....
(From a Greek fairy tale)

Since no other girl has succeeded in making the same transformation, marzipan figures are now usually eaten up at once.

Pine Nut Crescents

*7 oz. almonds (200 g)
8 oz. sugar (230 g)
3 ½ oz. egg whites (100 g).

pine nut seeds
rosewater

Combine in a heat-resistant casserole:
blanched and finely ground,

Stir over very low heat until bottom
becomes visible. When cool, shape little
crescents, roll in
brush with
and bake until golden yellow.

Bake on center rack	Temperature 350°F(180°C)	Baking time 10-15 min.	Store in glass jars

Orange Marzipan Rounds

9 oz. almond paste (250 g).
3 oz. conf. sugar (80 g)
2 Tbs orange spirit*
*1 unsprayed orange.

orange marmalade.
7 oz. chocolate coating (200 g),

*orange rind.

Put onto a cool surface (no wooden board):
Sift and add:

and at last, the super-thinly shredded rind of
Shape rolls 1 ¾ " thick and 3" long.
Hollow out lengthwise with an apple
corer and fill the cavity with firm
Cut off slices 1/5" thick. Melt
cover the rounds and sprinkle
with shredded
Store in glass jars.

Stuffed Dates (Photo p. 93)

10 ½ oz. dates (300 g).

4 ½ oz. almond paste (125 g)
2 ½ oz. conf. sugar (60 g)
1 Tbs apricot brandy.
*2 Tbs pistachios.

unsweetened chocolate.

Slice lengthwise and pit

Knead for filling:

Chop and add
Form a roll 1/2" in Ø and fill dates with mixture.
Flatten edges and dip the end into melted
Dry on wire rack. Store in glass jars.

Frankfurter Bethmännchen

*13 ½ oz. almonds (375 g)
12 ½ oz. conf. sugar (350 g)
3 Tbs rosewater.

Combine in a heat-resistant saucepan:
blanched, dried and ground twice

Stir over low heat until a lump forms. When
slightly cooled, add and knead in, onto a
cool surface:

1 oz. potato flour (30 g)
3 oz. conf. sugar (80 g)
1 dash of salt
2 small egg whites.

Shape a roll 1" in Ø. Cut off uniform slices. Form
nut-sized balls and flatten bottoms. Brush with

egg white
almonds.

and stud the sides with 3 blanched

Pinch slightly together at the top to obtain the
typical »Bethmännchen« shape. Place on split

oblaten.

Dry overnight. Bake until almonds are slightly
browned. Glaze thinly. For the glaze, sift
and beat with

7 oz. conf. sugar (200 g)
2 Tbs rose water
2 Tbs hot water

until well blended.

Bake on center rack	Temperature 480°F (250°C)	Baking time 5 min.	Store in glass jars

Macaroon Rings

7 oz. almond paste (200 g)
7 ½ oz. sugar (210 g)
1 cold egg white

Beat with dough-hooks of electric mixer:

to a smooth paste. Fill into pastry bag with star
shaped tip (4/5" in Ø) and place wreaths on round

oblaten (2 ½" in Ø).
redcurrant jelly.

After baking, fill centers with heated
Taste best when fresh.

Bake on top shelf	Temperature 375°F (190°C)	Baking time 4 min.	Store in tin

Zürich Leckerli

	Combine in a heat-resistant bowl:
*1 lb + 1 oz. almonds (480 g)	blanched, completely dried and superfinely ground
*7 bitter almonds (20 g),	prepared as above, and sifted
1 lb + 2 oz. conf. sugar (500 g).	Stir these ingredients in the bowl set into a saucepan with simmering water.
	Add
3 egg whites	and some
orange blossom water	until mixture forms a smooth paste. On a surface dusted with conf. sugar quickly knead in
1 egg yolk.	Divide paste. Roll out one half 1/3" thick and spread with smoothed
apricot jam.	Roll out other half of paste 1/3" thick, press leckerli molds into the paste, place on layer spread with apricot jam and cut out. If you have no wooden molds, cut out small squares with jagging wheel. Brush with rosewater. Let dry for 2 days on board dusted with conf. sugar. Bake on foil-lined cookie sheet. Glaze while still hot. For glaze sift:
7 oz. conf. sugar (200 g)	add and stir with
1 Tbs lemon juice	
1 Tbs Pflümli (plum brandy)	until smooth. Taste best when fresh.

Bake on top shelf	Temperature 375°F(190°C)	Baking time 5-8 min.	Store in glass jars

Rum Globes

	Cream:
3 oz. butter (80 g)	with
1 egg yolk.	Melt
7 oz. semisweet chocolate (200 g)	
	let cool, mix with butter mixture and
2 Tbs rum.	Chill. Shape cherry-sized globes. Roll in
chocolate shot	and store in glass jars in cool place.

Marzipan Potatoes

7 oz. almond paste (200 g)
5 ½ oz. conf. sugar (150 g)
1 Tbs rosewater

cocoa strongly de-oiled.

Combine:

and knead well. Shape rolls the thickness of a finger. Cut off cherry-sized pieces, shape balls, place in soup plate and sprinkle with sifted

Cover with another soup plate and shake. Impale with a wooden pick for »eyes« and slash »peel« slightly with a knife. Store in glass jars. Serve fresh. (Photo p. 163)

And this is what the recipe for Marzipan Potatoes looked like during the war:

Beat 2 oz. butter (62,5 g) with 7 oz. powdered sugar (200 g) until creamy. Mix with ½ vial bitter almond-substitute, 3 tablespoons skimmed milk and 9 oz. semolina (250 g). Roll in cocoa (if available!) or in a cinnamon-substitute and then let dry.

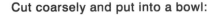

Apricot Slices

1 lb + 2 oz. dried apricots
(500 g).

2 Tbs apricot liquor

6 ½ oz. sugar (180 g)

4 oz. conf. sugar (120 g)
6 ½ oz. almond paste (180 g)

egg white
1/2 pistachio.

Cut coarsely and put into a bowl:

Sprinkle with
and let soak for at least 2 hours. Then
combine with
Send through meat grinder twice or mash with
blender. Shape mixture into an oblong bar
2 x 1 ½ " with a large wet metal spatula.
Sift
add
and knead until paste is smooth and light.
Roll out an oblong 1/5" thick and wrap around
bar. Seal seams firmly. Wrap in foil and refrigerate for one day.

With a wet, sharp knife cut off slices 1/6" thick.
You may dot the centers with some
and top each slice with

Store in a cool place in tightly closed containers
between sheets of parchment paper.
(Photo p. 93)

Apricot Confection

7 oz. dried apricots (200 g)
(best quality).
*3 ½ oz. almonds (100 g).

3 ½ oz. semisweet chocolate
(100 g).

Place on a wire rack:

Blanch and roast very lightly
Stud each apricot with 1 almond. (See illustration). Melt in double-boiler

Press almond against apricot and dip one third
into chocolate. Allow to dry well on wire rack
before storing confection in a glass jar or
porcelain container. (Photo opposite page)

Photo:
Apricot Confection

Quince »Cheese«

Deservedly most popular for decorating Christmas platters.

Important: Do not prepare too small a quantity as it would not be worth the effort. Too large a quantity at the same time is tiresome.

5,5 lb quinces (2500 g), With a wet cloth wipe the fuzz from remove stems and blossoms, wash and place in a large pot with cold water. Quinces need not be fully immersed. Cook until soft. Peel and core. Purée very finely with a blender or pass through a fine-eyed sieve. Weigh the pulp to

2,2 lb quince pulp (1000 g) add
2,2 lb granulated sugar (1000 g)
1 small ladle of the liquid. Boil at moderate heat stirring constantly until the bottom of the pot can bee seen and until the mixture drops in lumps from wooden spoon. A simpler method is to fill the sugar-pulp-mass into a flat ovenproof pan and let simmer in the oven at medium heat on center rack.

All you have to do is to scrape the sides occasionally and stir. Using either method, the finished product is a nice, glossy red-brown paste. Fill 1/2 - 1/3 " high into a ovenproof pan rinsed with water. Smooth quince paste with a spatula and allow to dry. Depending on room temperature and consistency, paste may dry within one day. Dip a sharp knife into cold water and cut quince »cheese« in 3/4" cubes. You may roll the cubes in sugar crystals or fill mass into copper molds and unmold by inverting.

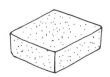
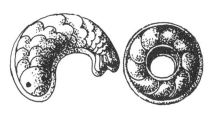

Storage: In glass jars or porcelain containers.
A praline box with molded bottom will produce attractive designs.
Important: let the cubes dry bevore storing! If properly stored, quince cubes will taste great, even after a year. (Photo p. 93)

Chestnut Confection

2 ½ oz. butter (60 g).
*12 ½ oz. chestnuts (350 g).

Brown slightly and let cool:
Roast and skin while hot:
Put through a meatgrinder twice or purée in
a blender.
Combine and cream the cold butter with

2 ½ oz. sugar (60 g)
2 Tbs vanilla sugar*
2 Tbs kirsch.

Add the chestnuts
and work all ingredients to a smooth paste.
Shape chestnut-sized balls, flatten sides and
bottoms slightly and place on aluminum foil.

Melt in double-boiler:
2 oz. milk-chocolate (50 g)
2 oz. semisweet chocolate (50 g)

Coat chestnuts leaving a small circle
on the bottoms. Let dry on wire rack.
Place in praline paper cups, store in a cool
place. May be consumed soon.

Sesame Crunch

2 ½ oz. sesame seeds (60 g).
2 ½ oz. brown sugar (60 g)
1 ½ oz. butter (40 g)
3 Tbs honey.

Roast lightly in a pan and put on a plate:
Combine in the pan:

and
Stir at moderate heat to a caramelized paste.
Blend in sesame seeds. Brush aluminum foil
with

almond oil,

and spread out the sesame paste 1/8" thick.
Cut into small rectangles before cooling and
bend them quickly lengthwise with a wooden
spoon handle. (See drawing). Sesame crunch
may be stored in glass jars for several months.

Heinerle

In a heat-resistant double-boiler melt

9 oz. coconut butter, Palmin
  (250 g)
9 oz. bitter chocolate
  (250 g)

(top quality and broken into pieces).
Set bowl aside. Stir in

9 oz. sugar (250 g)

(Do not use powdered sugar!) Add the scraped
seeds of a whole

vanilla bean.

When cooled beat in thoroughly until well
combined

4 whole eggs.
24 oblong oblaten.

Spread chocolate mass evenly on
Place side by side and let dry slightly.
Stack until about 1/2 - 3/4" high. Cover last
layer with an unspread

oblate.

Roll in parchment paper or aluminum foil and
weigh down with a heavy book and chill for

2-3 days in refrigerator. Cut into small neat rhombuses about 1/2" wide and 1 ½ "
long. Store in cool dry place in a tightly closed tin or glass jar.
»Lock up« if there is a sweet tooth about! (Photo p. 93)

Ice Confection, Ice Chocolate

Melt in double-boiler:

9 oz. coconut butter, (Palmin)
  (250 g).

Sift and add:

1 lb + 2 oz. conf. sugar (500 g)
4 ½ oz. dark cocoa (125 g)
1 Tbs genuine vanilla sugar*.

Beat until smooth and well combined. Fill (while
hot) into small molds rinsed with cold water
allowing them to harden in freezer. Unmold.
Ice chocolate will melt on your tongue! Must be
stored in refrigerator!

Genuine Pischinger Slices

4 ½ oz. softened butter (125 g)
4 ½ oz sugar (125 g)
3 egg yolks

*4 ½ oz. semisweet chocolate
  (125 g)
2 Tbs dark cocoa
seeds of ½ vanilla bean.

Karlsbad wafers.

chocolate coating

Beat:

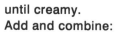

until creamy.
Add and combine:

finely grated,
sifted, and the
Spread mixture thinly and evenly on round unfilled
Place 3 wafers on top of each other and cover with parchment paper, or foil. Weigh down and chill overnight. With a sharp knife, cut out wedges (like small pieces of a tart) and cover with melted
and allow to dry in a draft - free place.
Store in glass jars or porcelain containers.

Carolas Pischinger

6 oblong oblaten.

Prepare chocolate paste as above, spreading evenly on
Weigh down and cut into 1-1 ½ " rectangles.
Store in glass jars in a cool place. Delicious!

Blackamoor Balls

*3 ½ oz. hazelnuts (100 g)	Put into a mixing bowl:
3 ½ oz. sugar (100 g)	slightly roasted and ground
1 egg yolk	
1 tsp flour or cornstarch	and (according to taste)
80 % proof rum.	Blend all ingredients thoroughly. Shape small balls the size of a cherry.
	Melt in double-boiler:
3 ½ oz. fine unsweetened chocolate (100 g)	or prepare
chocolate icing (p. 114).	Roll balls first in icing, then in
sugar crystals.	Place on baking sheet lined with aluminum foil and let dry in »slow oven«. If you bake in gas oven, leave door open completely.

Bake on	Temperature	Baking time	Store in
center rack	270°F(140°C)	10-15 min.	glass jars

Chocolate Truffles

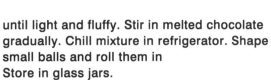

6 ½ oz. bitter orange chocolate (180 g).	Melt in double-boiler:
	Let cool.
	Cream:
3 ½ oz. butter (100 g)	
6 ½ oz. conf. sugar (180 g)	
3 egg yolks	until light and fluffy. Stir in melted chocolate gradually. Chill mixture in refrigerator. Shape small balls and roll them in
chocolate shot.	Store in glass jars.

Hazelnut Clusters

Bring to a boil in a heavy pan:

2 oz. butter (50 g)
2 oz. honey (50 g)
5 ½ oz. brown sugar (150 g)
1 Tbs vanilla sugar*
½ cup heavy cream.

Stirring constantly until mixture thickens
and is lightly brown. Blend in:

*6 Tbs candied fruits (60 g)   chopped
*7 oz. hazelnuts (200 g)   whole and skinned.

With 2 teaspoons, drop onto a floured cookie
sheet »little mountains« well apart from one
another. Bake for 3 min., then pat into shape
with a liqueur glass. Return to oven for another
2 minutes. Cool on wire rack. Brush backside
with melted

chocolate coating.   Allow to dry at room temperature. (Photo p. 93).

Bake on	Temperature	Baking time	Store in
top shelf	350°F(180°C)	5 min.	glass jars

Blackamoor Kisses

Combine and stir thoroughly:

*5 ½ oz. hazelnuts (150 g) or
*5 ½ oz. almonds (150 g)   unblanched and ground,
1 ½ egg whites
5 ½ oz. sugar (150 g).

Knead well. The best method is to knead with
the dough-hooks of an electric mixer. Shape
small buns, place on buttered sheet and bake
very slowly. Kisses must be soft inside. When
cooled completely, coat with the following
chocolate icing. Bring to a boil:

1/8 cup water   add
2 oz. unsweetened chocolate
   (50 g)   broken into pieces
5 ½ oz. sugar cubes (150 g).   Blend well.
                               Apply when lukewarm.

Bake on	Temperature	Baking time	Store in
center rack	300-325°F(150-180°C)	10 min.	glass jars

Chocolate Carolines

Cream until very fluffy:

4 ½ oz. softened butter (125 g)
9 oz. sugar (250 g).

Stir in

*9 oz. semisweet chocolate
    (250 g)
*9 oz. almonds (250 g)

finely grated
unblanched and ground.
Whip until stiff

4 egg whites.
10 ½ oz. flour (300 g).

Sift and blend lightly into the creamed mixture
Let dough rest for 1 hour in a cool place.
Roll out 1/2" thick, cut out rounds and bake
on foil. Cool completely, coat with white
icing. You may garnish carolines with

chocolate piping.

For icing: sift and beat together:

7 oz. conf. sugar (200 g)
2 Tbs arrack
1 Tbs hot water

until thick and creamy. (10 min.)
For piping,
melt in a double-boiler:

1 ½ oz. chocolate (40 g).
1 Tbs sugar.

Add and combine
When lightly cooled, fill into small parchment
piping bag, cut off tip and apply chocolate
onto white icing. (Photo p. 73).

Bake on center rack	Temperature 375°F(190°C)	Baking time 15 min.	Store in glass jars

181

Almond Splinters

Melt in a large frying pan:

1 Tbs honey
1 Tbs butter.

Add

*10 oz. almonds (280 g)

(blanched and slivered) and let caramelize slightly. Blend in the superfinely shredded rind of

1 unsprayed orange,
2 Tbs rum
*6 Tbs candied lemon peel (60 g)
*5 Tbs candied orange peel (50 g)

and
both finely slivered.
Melt in a double-boiler

13 ½ oz. semisweet chocolate (380 g)

combine with almond mixture. Place mounds on buttered or oiled aluminum foil. Decorate tops with some very thin shreds of

unsprayed orange peel.

Let harden - the quickest way is to place splinters in freezer. Store in glass jars or porcelain containers.
This confection may also be prepared with

milk chocolate.

Toffees

Combine in a wide heavy pan
and stir over medium heat:

1 ½ cup heavy cream
½ cup raw milk
1 tsp butter
1 lb sugar (455 g)
1 Tbs vanilla sugar*

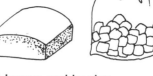

almond oil
(no bitter almond oil).

until mixture is light brown and begins to thicken. Pour onto a sheet or ovenproof pan brushed with

Smooth with a spatula. Let set, mark into cubes 3/4 x 3/4" with a knife. When cooled, cut apart. That's how toffees get the »cushion« shape.

Florentines

2 oz. butter (60 g)
2 oz. honey (60 g)
3 ½ oz. brown sugar (100 g)
1 Tbs vanilla sugar*.
½ cup heavy cream.

*5 oz. almonds (140 g)
*3 ½ oz. hazelnuts (100 g)
*3 oz. candied cherries (80 g)
  red and green
*4 Tbs candied lemon peel (40 g)
*4 Tbs candied orange peel (40 g)

5 ½ oz. semisweet chocolate
  (150 g).

Bring to a boil in a heavy
wide pan:

At last add
Let simmer until mixture
begins to thicken. Add
blanched and slivered,
ground

coarsely chopped,

both finely chopped. Stir well. With
2 teaspoons drop batter widely spaced on
waxed cookie sheet. Bake for 5 min. Then
use a glass as a guide to shape again.
Bake until rounds begin to brown. Transfer
to a wire rack with spatula or thin bladed
knife. Brush the bottoms of the slightly
cooled florentines twice with melted

Draw lines with a fork. Dry in a warm room.

Bake on top shelf	Temperature 350°F(180°C)	Baking time 8-10 min.	Store in glass jars

Mocha Truffles

2 oz. butter (50 g)
1 egg yolk.
½ Tbs vanilla extract.
3 ½ oz. conf. sugar (100 g)
2 Tbs cocoa.
*5 oz. mocha chocolate (140 g)

conf. sugar.
1 choco mocha bean.

Cream until foamy:

Stir in
Sift together and add:

Melt in a double-boiler and let cool
Stir into the creamed mixture. With 2 teaspoons form and set truffles on foil and
refrigerate or freeze until hard. Dust with
sifted
Garnish each truffle with:
Keep refrigerated in glass jars or porcelain
containers.

Recipes of my Friends

French Biscuits   *from Mrs. Erika Liefland*

Sift onto a board 1 lb + 2 oz. flour (500 g) and 5 ½ oz. conf. sugar (150 g).
Add 12 ½ oz. very cold butter and knead to a smooth dough. Shape rolls
about 1 ½ " in Ø. Chill overnight. Then cut off 1/8" slices and bake
until set but not brown for about 12 min. at 350°F (180°C). Exquisite cookies!

Xmas Barlets   *from Mrs. Hilde Bieber*

Combine and beat 9 oz. butter (250 g), 9 oz. sugar (250 g) and 6 eggs.
Fold in 9 oz. grated chocolate (250 g), 3 ½ oz shaved almonds (100 g), as
well as 7 oz. ground almonds (200 g) and 3 ½ oz. sifted flour (100 g).
Spread batter onto a well buttered cookie sheet and bake for 25 minutes
at 375°F (190°C). Coat with chocolate icing (p. 114) or melted chocolate coating.
Cut into bars or squares immediately so that icing cannot crack!
Easy to make and yet delicious!

My own Recipes

My own Recipes

Alphabetical List of Recipes

Die feinsten **PLÄTZCHEN-REZEPTE** gesammelt von Olli Leeb
German Edition of «my favorite COOKIES from the Old Country«
190 p.   ISBN 3-921799-98-8

BAVARIAN COOKING assembled by Olli Leeb
Over 300 recipes of Old Bavaria, Franconia and Swabia, easy to prepare at home.
Aside from typical Bavarian specialities please note information about Bavaria,
the Bavarians and their customs. A schedule of activities in Bavaria, written in
easily understandable language, is provided. Also included you will find color
photos and numerous illustrations.   172 p.   ISBN 3-921799-85-6

BAYERISCHE LEIBSPEISEN zusammengetragen von Olli Leeb
German Edition of »Bavarian Cooking«. 172 p. ISBN 3-921799-80-5

Garment Care by Olli Leeb
Stain Removal easy made.
English Edition of »Der Fleck muß weg!«   80 Seiten   ISBN 3-921 799-83-X

Kochbuch-Verlag Olli Leeb   D-80687 München